About the Author - My Story

Even though I had been in the landscaping business in my earlier years, my introduction to Artificial Grass resulted from my wife and I purchasing a new home with very large areas for landscaping. We decided to put in a putting green. It was so amazing to me how Artificial Grass looked and felt so real; however, I was even more impressed with all the savings I was realizing in time and money for maintenance. What a tremendous product which I quickly started showing to all my friends and acquaintances. Soon they were all installing Artificial Grass in their homes.

I spent time on those installation projects carefully watching each step of the installation projects and then I started helping friends and neighbors to install their Artificial Grass. Before I realized it, I was booked solid for several months with installation jobs. So I launched into the business and was able to grow to the point of employing groups of installers and acquiring my own dump trucks and tractors.

Artificial Grass is so surprising to customers how lush and appealing it is compared to the early days of "astro turf." At the time the business was growing, my wife was being certified as a contractor and learning about Green-Environmentally friendly building standards. She started to introduce me to all the benefits Artificial Grass offers in helping conserve earth's water resources and help stop the polluting of water supplies. When I initially started installing Artificial Grass it was because I was so amazed at how Artificial Grass can make such a difference on the appeal and appearance of landscaping. After learning and understanding how much it benefits the environment as well, I became even more passionate about getting more Artificial Grass installed.

After several years of contracting, our company started selling a lot of grass to other contractors. Soon I found myself helping other contractors calling me for advice. The wholesale sales part of my business was getting as large as the installation part. As a result I had contractors constantly calling me from all parts of the country asking for installation guidance.

It became difficult to work on installation jobs since I was so busy consulting our wholesale contractors. I remember one time trying to start a seaming on a job and getting call after call from my wholesale customers.

As a result, I started teaching large classes where contractors could pay $200 to come and train with me for several days on installing the Artificial Grass. The word got out about my training classes and in 2006, I was approached by a large landscaping company, John Deere Landscape, to train their contractors and customers in proper Artificial Grass installation. Soon I was teaching large workshops and traveling all around the country helping contractors. Many times I was being flown to jobsites in Montana, Florida and Texas to help with problems. I met many people who had developed the same passion for Artificial Grass as me.

This book is inspired by the many hours I have spent learning how to do an excellent job installing Artificial Grass and also spending many more hours showing homeowners and contractors how to do the same. The records for John Deere show that I have trained literally thousands of contractors in their training classes. I am also inspired by watching people respond with amazement and satisfaction at their new installation; just as I did my first time. Finally, I have a great sense of pride to be helping to develop an industry that has some great solutions for the issues of protecting the earth's water resources and pollution that is plaguing most all water sources.

I encourage you to take full advantage of my years of experience and get your Artificial Grass lawn installed and even consider using Part 2 of this book and becoming a professional installer and joining this great industry with me. Also, to assure your satisfaction with this book and great success installing or launching a business installing, I want to make myself available to you for your comments and questions.

To get my assistance be sure and reach me at:
bob@ArtificialGrassLiquidators.com

Thank you for getting this book

Bob Delozier

Acknowledgments

I would like to give special thanks to some people who have been very supportive to me in making this book become a reality.

Many thanks to my Wife and Family, Will Grissom, Tony Vena and Greg Barela for their contributions.

And to the thousands of contractors who I have met over the years; who have come to my training classes and workshops; and learned how to install Artificial Grass properly.

Thank you for all your support.

Bob Delozier

Intentionally Left Blank

TABLE OF CONTENTS

INTRODUCTION

For many decades, grass lawns have been installed in our homes, parks, and commercial areas to create those beautiful places we meet to enjoy and relax with people. Whether in a public park, private country club, or our back yard; every culture values these grassy landscapes. But the time has come in the history of our planet to take a close look at the real costs our real grass lawns have on the environment and the  contribution it makes to polluting or depleting our water supply. In 2008, Sam Bozzo directed a documentary called "Blue Gold" which fully describes the coming crisis developing regarding water resources.

With many conversations about the environment the solutions often mean there will be hard sacrifices and the need for making expensive and inconvenient changes to change our future. When it comes to the issue of Natural Grass, I am excited to share how Artificial Grass is a perfect alternative with far more benefits and value.

When it comes to the harsh environmental impact of grass lawns and landscapes the solutions will mean far better grass landscapes with numerous benefits. Let me share that when I first installed the Artificial Grass I was not very aware of all the benefits to conservation and the natural ecology.

This book is born out of my desire to see homeowners be convinced that they can see all the benefits of Artificial Grass in their own yards. I want this book to help owners avoid installation mistakes and new installers  make mistakes in successfully operating their businesses. It is my hope that homeowners will get to have that great experience that so many of my customers have had through the years of seeing the dramatic appeal of Artificial Grass and spend a great deal more time enjoying their yards rather than spending the time and money maintaining the yard.

In Part One, I will give any homeowner a Roadmap and Simple Guide to install the Artificial Turf at their own home. The following installation techniques were developed from many years of successfully installing Artificial Grass in a variety of conditions and designs. You will be able to benefit from that experience; bypass the frustrating trial and error of many home improvements; and properly install your Artificial Grass.

In Part Two, I want to provide help for those who would want to install Artificial Grass as a business. The Artificial Grass industry is a very promising and fulfilling industry to join. I want to help develop a sound business strategy and plan for quickly launching profitably into this wonderful industry.

I want this book to become a great resource for both the homeowner and the new Artificial Grass installer. Additionally, I want to be available to be contacted with questions so that you will be successful.

Like me, you may install an Artificial Grass lawn in your home and be so captivated that you may want to do the same for others and be in the business. In Part Two I have laid out a game plan for you to effectively and profitably start installing Artificial Grass for others.

I am so confident with the guidance and roadmap that I am providing. I would be glad to extend the invitation to contact me with questions and comments you may have to:

Bob@ArtificialGrassLiquidators.com

AMAZING BENEFITS OF ARTIFICIAL GRASS

Artificial Grass will give you AMAZING BENEFITS in 4 Key Ways:

1)**Natural Look and Feel** of Real Grass with Incredible Durability
2)**Realize Time and Money Savings** with Artificial Grass' Low Maintenance

3)**Special features** you cannot even get with Natural Grass …. Like eliminating mud prints or grass stains
4)Be Responsible with **Earth-Friendly Benefits**

1) Natural Look and Feel — But Incredibly Durable

Today's Artificial Turf is made to give you a <u>Soft and Real</u> Grass look <u>and</u> to last for a decade or more. Also, you will not see fading or dead grass spots during these years. Whether you are in a rainy or dry climate you will not need to deal with the brown spots or moldy black spots.. Artificial Grass is porous and can drain without any problems. You will not have to let the fields dry out; that means you will have more usable days for sports activities with Artificial Grass.

Over the course of two decades, you or your paid landscape company will be spending a lot of money and time doing some combination of Aerating; Dethatching; Dead-Spot Replacing; Leveling Bumps and Depressions; and even doing a Total Renovation or Re-installation of your grass. Artificial Grass will not require any of these services. Also, your new

Artificial Grass lawn will be able to stand up to the wear and tear of heavy foot traffic and your pet's digging habits.

Artificial Grass will not require any of these expensive and painstaking processes any longer. That means when you are doing a fair comparison of the cost of an Artificial Grass installation you should realistically look at the cost of repairing and replacing your grass lawn area <u>2 or 3 times</u>!

Also, unlike natural grass, Artificial Grass should be seen as a valuable asset, similar to fine carpets or awnings, when you are selling or valuating your home. It will certainly be a great addition to the natural aesthetics and curb appeal of your home.   Rich green and fresh looking grass all year round.

I will show you a great cost comparison later; first, let us look at some other *AMAZING BENEFITS!*

2) Realize Time and Money Savings

Water Usage: Since many homes use as much as half of their water irrigating landscape you will not be paying for all that water month after month. Be free to take a trip and not worry about watering the lawn.

Low Maintenance: Whether you maintain your own yard or pay a landscaper, you will not need to mow, edge or trim your lawn again. You will spend a <u>small fraction</u> of the time maintaining your new Artificial Grass lawn. Put you mower up for sale ! You will not be buying or repairing anymore lawn equipment either.

If you or your relative's health or age does not allow them to be active in the yard; Artificial Grass is the perfect solution. Many of my clients use all that extra time and money to work on their "wish lists." Instead of mowing, you can make that rose or herb garden a reality!

So you will not need to worry about the dull brown patches in your lawn any longer; and you can start using your extra time for other landscape projects.

Chemicals and Treatments: You will not be spending money and time treating your lawn to protect you from pests, weeds, fungus, and molds. Cleaning and disinfecting your Artificial Grass is quick and easy.

Rebates: Many water districts and cities have been trying to induce water conservation by offering rebates to those who will install water friendly landscaping. You should check your local area for applicable rebates; but here are some examples. In Reno, Nevada there was a $1 per square foot offered for removing natural grass. In Cash-Strapped California there were rebates of 30 cents per square foot offered in San Diego and Los Angeles.   You will certainly be able to expect more incentives as the issue of water shortages or pollution continue to be key issues with politicians.

Now I would like to talk about some special BENEFITS and Unique qualities of Artificial Grass where Natural Grass just can not compare!

3) Special Benefits of Artificial Grass

You can Install Artificial Grass virtually Anywhere! Your landscape designs can be very flexible and creative with Artificial Grass since you can revitalize your yard by covering damaged concrete or wood decks. For instance you can create layers and steps that can be covered with Artificial Grass..

Reclaim your Backyard from Bugs, Flies, and other Pests!   Unless you do a lot of spraying with expensive, water-polluting chemicals; your Natural Grass will be a great nesting area for fleas, tics, flies, bees, etc. This can limit your enjoyment; lounging, playing or eating in your yard can be especially difficult. Also, your pets are always needing to be protected against the targeted for flea and tic infestation.

AMAZING BENEFITS OF ARTIFICIAL GRASS

Finally a "Grass" Lawn for those with Allergies or Pollens!   For those who have relatives or friends that are sensitive to outdoor grasses, Artificial Grass may be a great option.

No muddy prints in your house! During wet times of the year; your Artificial Grass will drain off water, eliminating those muddy areas that can be tracked into your home.

Stop cleaning grass stains on your clothes!   Artificial Grass will not be leaving those green streaks on clothes after playing on it.

Soft and Safe Surface for your little Athletes! Artificial Grass can be designed to create a "Soft Fall" surface. This means that as you and your kids are playing there is much better impact absorption. This means less wear and tear on the joints and reduction of injuries. This is why the sports industry has widely implemented Artificial Grass solutions.

Create Green Areas where there is high-foot traffic or even auto traffic! Areas out by your curb or in driveways are often concrete or rock because natural grass will not stand up to the high amount of traffic. Artificial Grass is designed with the right durability. In commercial areas there are often grass areas that should be converted to Artificial Grass. One great benefit, also, is

that you will not need to have maintenance crews working around these crowded areas.

Artificial Grass can be great for Erosion control! When there are areas of landscape where frequent water flow can drain causing the soil to erode away; you should consider using Artificial Grass for covering and protecting those areas. Artificial Grass is an excellent way to beautify those areas while protecting the soil from draining off.

More easily keep pet areas sanitary and allow everyone to enjoy your clean and fresh backyard grass areas! Even though our "furry family members" are so valuable to us; their bathroom can often ruin the backyard and attract a lot of flies and smells that make it impossible for other family members to enjoy. Artificial Grass can quickly and easily be decontaminated and areas of your lawn can be fitted with In-fill that limits odors. This makes Artificial Grass ideal for allowing pets to use the back yard without taking it over.

4) **Artificial Grass is part of the answer for Water Conservation and Pollution Issues**

Conservation: During my years in the Artificial Grass industry it has been a great joy to know that I am part of the solution to some issues that are affecting our environments. In dry areas where water is more scarce Artificial Grass is a key answer to allowing for pleasant green landscapes without the need for large water usage. In California, where I live, it was estimated that in one year the Artificial Grass installations had eliminated the need to use 720 million gallons of water for irrigating. That large savings will carry over and increase year after year.

Some areas of the U.S. have plenty of water resources. However, water prices in those areas do continue to rise at a faster rate than in dry areas. So the need to conserve is still a key issue for homeowners and government users alike.

According to the Department of Agriculture, grass lawns are the largest "crop" in the United States and very likely the same is true around the industrialized world. It is exciting to me that by installing Artificial Grass we are freeing up those water resources for other uses.

Pollution: To keep natural lawns maintained it is necessary to spray regularly with many varieties of chemicals. For many years those chemicals are

AMAZING BENEFITS OF ARTIFICIAL GRASS

leeching into the water tables or flowing into storm drains and contaminating other water sources.. Because Artificial Grass eliminates the need for these chemicals, it is one great solution to start to turn this issue around. Furthermore, Artificial Grass installations are even part of the cleaning of water moving into the water tables. The use of base materials in Artificial Grass installations actually act as a Bio-Filtration system for water that soaks through the grass into the water table.

Lowering the Need for Gas Engine Equipment: Because of the huge inventory of natural grass lawns there is the need for armies of landscape crews to run gas-powered mower, edgers and trimmers. One study showed that the average lawn will have as much as 13 gallons of gasoline spilled on it during the year of maintenance. Also, one mowing can pollute the area as much as a 100 mile trip in the car. Artificial Grass installation reduces the need for all the maintenance and consequently the emissions of pollutants caused by the maintenance equipment.

Green Job Creation: As the need for water conservation becomes more pressing, Artificial Grass installations will increase and there will be greater demand for workers in all phases of the industry. The Artificial Grass manufacturers, installers and maintenance industry will be able to absorb workers from the natural grass industry.

The Artificial Grass Industry is becoming very conscious of conservation. As Artificial Grass lawns that are being replaced due to age; one company has been able to use those turfs for creating Biofuels used in manufacturing turf. This helps with ozone gases and the burden on landfills. On the other hand, natural grass trimmings have overwhelmed the landfills and are partly responsible for creating "greenhouse" gasses emitted from landfills.

Look at these Great "BEFORE and AFTER" Results!

AMAZING BENEFITS OF ARTIFICIAL GRASS

Look at these Great "BEFORE and AFTER" Results!

Since ARTIFICIAL GRASS has so many BENEFITS, Let us get started installing your new Artificial Grass lawn Now!

Intentionally Left Blank

Part 1

PROPERLY INSTALLING
ARTIFICIAL GRASS

PART 1: PROPERLY INSTALLING ARTIFICIAL GRASS

In this part of the book I want to organize and give you a plan for each of the steps you will take to get your lawn installed. There are five major steps to properly installing your new lawn. First, I will guide you through the steps for designing and planning the lawn. Then you will be ready to purchase your supplies and gather the right tools and equipment. Now you will be ready to be instructed and guided through each of the major steps of the installation process. Those three major steps are:

- Preparing your site
- Cutting and Laying the Artificial Grass and In-Filling
- Final Brushing and Finishing the Project

At each step I have provided easy to read instructions, forms and checklists that will allow you to have the confidence that you are prepared to complete that major step and start the next step. Also, I have provided an email in the Introduction Section for you to contact me and let me know if you have questions I can help you with.

I am looking forward to hearing about your successful installation. In fact, it would be a good idea if you would take some "Before" pictures of your yard so you can see the difference and appreciate what an impact Artificial Grass has made in beautifying your home.

Overview of Installing Artificial Grass at your home:

Before we get started with the first step of designing the layout of your new lawn, I would like to take you through an overview of the process. You should plan several days of work for you and a helper. If you have a typical 800 square foot back yard to install, you and one helper should be ready to use two weekends finishing the installation.

In the next chapters I plan to guide you step by step through the details. Here are the stages you can anticipate for properly installing your lawn:

- Remove all existing grass or other vegetation down to the root system. If there is only dirt where you are installing than make sure to remove large rocks and level or balance that area.

- With the use of a framing material you will outline the areas for your grass. This becomes the mold that you will use for the next step.

- Lay down a base aggregate material around the whole area where your grass will be installed.

- Compact that material or base and create a flat grade with the proper drainage levels.

- Cover the area and tack down a weed barrier

- Cut your Artificial Grass into the lengths you designed.

- Starting with the largest piece first, lay down and snug the Artificial Grass tight as you nail it down to the area outlined.

- Keep adding each Artificial Grass strip along the side of the other and properly hide the seams.

- Spread In-Fill materials and brush and soak them into the Artificial Grass to keep the fibers standing up and give your lawn weight and a "bounce."

- Final Clean up, vacuuming and clearing out any materials or nails.

Intentionally Left Blank

Step 1

DESIGN AND PLANNING YOUR

This first step is critical for assuring the success and easy installation of your Artificial Grass project. After you are completed with the Design and Planning stage of your project you will have determined four important details:

First, What is the primary use of the area where you are going to install Artificial Grass? This will help you choose the appropriate turf and assure that you will have many years enjoying your Artificial Grass lawn. I encourage you to "Start with the End in Mind."

This means you need to know clearly what the goals for the area you want to surface with Artificial Grass. Will there be a lot of foot traffic? What kind of look are you trying to achieve? Artificial Grass can add real appeal and that perfect lush grass look to Pool Areas, Pet Areas, Playground areas, unsightly concrete areas, and even Retaining Wall areas. As mentioned in the Benefits of Artificial Grass above; you can place Artificial Grass in areas where you have stone walk ways or other special trees and landscape features. So be creative and plan out carefully the Artificial Grass project areas.

Secondly, your drawing tells you how much area are you going to be covering with Artificial Grass and how many seams and cuts will you be creating between the Artificial Grass pieces for seaming. This will give you the information you need to purchase the right amount of supplies and get the tools required for the project.

Thirdly, what is the best elevation or grade of the Artificial Grass area and are there any special areas where there are trees or other landscaping to plan for? If you want to do a Putting Green I have included a special section in Part 2 of this book for installing a Putting Green.

Finally, how will the Artificial Grass area drain water effectively during times of large rainfall or rain runoff and what are the plans for any current sprinkler systems or irrigation lines? Your Design and Planning should start by making a written layout of your project. Use grid paper or our Form in back of this book and make a drawing of the area or site.

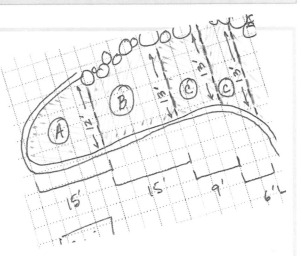

Measure the area and draw those dimensions on the drawing. See the example above. What you are focusing on is how many linear feet will be outlining the area you are going to install your Artificial Grass.

Use a flexible tape to take measurements and remember to allow for the rise and fall of the final grade by draping the tapes over the ground. Be sure to round up to the next linear foot when estimating for your materials or at least add some extra inches to your measurements..

When I use the word "Pattern" I am talking about the installation area. So by creating a diagram you can determine the turf needs. The key is to be able to purchase the appropriate amount to complete the job with the least amount of waste possible. So re-create the pattern on the ground with your tape measures. The pattern also indicates the seams, water, electricity, and other utilities. You will want to plan to redirect the irrigation to natural grass to other landscape areas or remove or cap off those lines. **Follow the instructions for irrigation very carefully— it can ruin your project!

Unless you have the necessary training and licensing; I would hire a proper contractor to handle any moving of electric or gas lines you find under the natural soil you are removing. If you are digging in Public Areas (front sidewalks) then be sure to notify your city or county authorities.

On your diagram you can use colors to note areas where there are Hard versus Soft Edges in the Patterns.

Hard Edges are perimeter edges of a synthetic grass installation project that touch elements that will not or cannot move; walkways, driveways, walls, patios, fences, buildings, foundations. The reason you are measuring and defining these Hard Edges is so you can plan for lining them with some materials that will assure a high quality finished look on those edges.

Soft Edges are landscape areas that do not connect or touch upon a hard, unmoving surface material such as a walkway, path, driveway, wall, fence line, or other surfaces such as field rocks. You will be able to be flexible in your cuts with Soft edges since you can plan to tuck the turf under rocks or other landscape materials.

Even though Artificial Grass is very durable and will provide you many years of excellent reliability; be sure and plan carefully for areas of your lawn that are heavily traveled. Just as with carpeting in your home; you will want to plan to put in walk areas or pathways so that those parts of your Artificial Grass lawn do not have advanced wear and tear.

Make sure and get a clearly drawn shape (or Pattern) with each line of the shape showing what the length of that part of the outline. Draw a shape on the drawing where there are any trees or other landscaping. You want to

show any breaks in the Artificial Grass area where there may be walkways or any other cemented areas. You may want to look at having several Artificial Grass areas. For instance, you may want to designate an area where you want to install a Putting Green or you may want a small strip where there is cement to have covered with grass. This drawing is the place to include all those details.

Now you will start to divide up your outline shape into rectangle and square shapes. The first thing you are trying to determine is what is the total linear feet of the outline of the shape you have drawn.

Tip: Since Artificial Grass is delivered in 15 foot widths; your short sides on those squares or rectangles can only have a maximum width of 15 feet. You will want to start create lengths starting with the Largest Space first.

This can be an Important Step! Since your Artificial Grass will come with a width of 15 feet; you can minimize the amount of turf needed by looking at designing your shapes in different directions. For example:

If you have a circle Pattern you want to look at the amount of turf pieces you will use running the Artificial Grass roll in different directions. Sometimes changing the direction can allow you to purchase less Artificial Grass or have fewer seams to work with. Be sure and play with the various options.

DESIGN AND PLANNING YOUR ARTIFICIAL GRASS LAWN

Quick Review of Square Feet and Linear Feet: Just in case you have been out of school a long time; if a shape has a Width of 12 feet and a length of 10 feet, then you will count that shape as (12 x 10) 120 square feet. So you add up all the shapes inside your outlined areas and this is the amount of Artificial Grass you will need to order.

Secondly, you want to take each of the shapes and determine the square footage of each shape. Make sure and divide the area or multiple outlined areas with the largest square and rectangle shapes possible. Laying out the large pieces of Artificial Turf goes quickly, while fitting and seaming is more time consuming. A well-planned pattern that was created to keep seaming at the minimum can help to save time because of fewer seams. Remember, you will need to cut into the Artificial Turf where you are allowing for trees or other landscape features. So you will need to plan for seams in those areas.

Tip: Even though Artificial Grass is very durable and should give you a good 10 years of enjoyment; you should be ordering an extra 50 square feet to keep for emergencies. This is the same concept used when you paint. You always keep some extra paint in case you may need to do some touching up. Artificial Grass does have the same issue of varying shades and you would be wise to keep a small remnant on hand in case, for instance, a barbecue fell on the lawn and did some damage.

Now you have the outline of your Artificial Grass area and you know the linear feet around the area and how much Artificial Grass you will need to cover each of the square or rectangle shapes you divided that area into.

Every place inside the outlined area where you have drawn a line to create a square or rectangle is a place where you will be cutting the Artificial Grass and creating a seam. I will be describing how to properly lay your grass so the seams are not visible.

However, since each of those seam areas will require extra work and supplies it is important to try to design your strips large enough to limit the number of seams the best as possible.

The total linear feet around the area where you have Hard Edges needs to be measured so that you will be able to purchase a durable edging material called Benderboard; which you will be installing to create the physical outline of your Artificial Grass area.

If your Project area has some large trees where there are roots that grow above the surface; you will want to plan for having Root Barriers to protect the Artificial Grass. Root Barriers run vertically and are very common at landscape supply stores.

So now we are ready to gather your materials and supplies.

Intentionally Left Blank

Step 2

Buy Your Artificial Grass and Gather Your Supplies and Tools

BUY YOUR ARTIFICIAL GRASS AND GATHER SUPPLIES

With your design in hand you are now ready to get all your supplies and tools that you will use on the project. You will want to move all back yard furniture or any items that will impede the project out of the area. You will need to have a Staging area for your tools and equipment. In the front of your home you will need to plan for an area for delivery of your Artificial Grass and Base.

Choosing your Artificial Grass: First, you will want to  choose a type that compliments the look in your neighborhood. Match your grass coloring and type to suit your neighboring lawn if that is applicable. Also, it is recommended that if you not choose a lighter colored turf with a darker colored roof.

Secondly, make sure that the style you use will accommodate the type of use. If you will have a lot of foot traffic or pets in the area then select an Artificial Turf for that purpose. However, if it is a low traffic area then you can economize on the durability and cost of your selection. It may make sense to use different types of turf in different parts of your project areas; discuss it with your supplier.

There are certainly plenty of choices for your Artificial Grass choice. There are turfs that simulates Bermuda, Fescue, Rye, St. Augustine's and plenty of color and texture variations. There are some characteristics of Artificial Grass that you will want to take note of:

Ounce Weight tells you how much yarn was used. The higher weights will be more durable. Most commonly I recommend a 70 ounce face weight; however, a 60 ounce can be okay if there are budgetary concerns.

Multi-colored, Dual Filament is a type of Artificial Grass I have recommended a lot. There are advantages to picking a turf with Thatch.

Thatch is a smaller twisted and curly yarn that is accumulated down by the backing and will help hold your in-fill well. Depending on the Thatch product there may be less In-Fill to purchase over the whole area you are installing. Finally, the Thatch seems to have a better rebound or bounce to it and the blades stay vertical better over time.

Weed Barrier: I would recommend that you purchase this covering to lay down just prior to laying out your Artificial Grass. You will be purchasing enough Weed Barrier to cover the square footage of the Pattern. Besides providing long lasting protection against weed growth; a Weed Barrier makes a good under cover when you are seaming your turf together. I also like to have the weed barrier on the surface because it helps provide a layer between the backing on your turf and the Base Layer you compact. At times certain backings can agitate against that Base Layer and cause a rock in the Base to pull loose. This can cause grade failure and leave soft spots or bumps in your lawn. Also, you will want to get your Root Barrier if your design calls for the turf to be around large tree roots.

Base: You will want to contact a local construction materials supplier to arrange to have a Decomposed Granite (DG) or Crushed Miscellaneous Base (CMB) delivered to your work site or front of your home. The supplier will want to know the area you are covering and how many inches you will be covering. Remember you will be compressing the base so you will need to order 3 to 4 inches. Order enough to raise the level in areas where large rocks or roots may have come out during the excavation of the project area.

Infill: After the lawn is laid you will be evenly spreading and brushing in some Infill material. The Infill will help the blades to stay vertical and can also add a "bounce" to the grass. There are several products you can use

You should consult your chosen supplier about your choices for an In-Fill that they know has a good performance record. If you want to do some research, I have some websites in the Manufactures and Suppliers Section. However, depending on your budget, you may want to use a more affordable Crum rubber or even clean play sand. If you purchased the Artificial Turf with Thatch you could plan on purchasing 1 to 3 pounds of Infill for every square foot of turf. If you choose a turf without Thatch than the supplier will have a recommended amount to follow.

Here are some approximations and budget guidelines for your Project:
- Artificial Grass: $2.00 up to $4.50 per square foot
- Base: Decomposed Granite at $1.65; CMB at 80 cents per square foot
- Weed Barrier: 7 to 10 cents per square foot
- InFill: Flex Sand at 35 cents; DuraFill or Crumb Rubber at 25 cents; and Clean Play Sand at approximately 10 cents per pound.

Now let us look at the supplies you will need and then the tools you will be using for your project.

- Flexible Tape Measure
- Snap line for marking long cuts of turf
- Hard-Edge Level – 2 to 4 foot (can also be used as straight edge for cutting small pieces of turf)
- Square or T-Square for squaring edges of turf
- Wheel barrows for moving the Base
- Flat head shovels
- Spades – Rounded head
- Large and small Picks for removing Natural Grass
- Leaf rake
- Asphalt or landscape rake

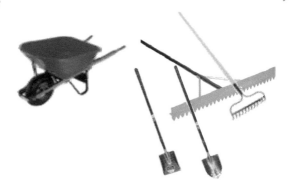

EQUIPMENT AND TOOLS

You will want to locate an equipment yard where you can rent these items on the days you are going to use them. Your first step of excavating a yard can be done with Picks and Shovels; however, the small expense of a Sod Cutter will certainly save a lot of time and effort. A Sod Cutter can cut away existing lawn areas, their root systems and any other type of ground cover; easily and quickly.

Once you are ready to spread or compact your base you will want to rent these three items:

- 2" x 4" or Larger Piece of Wood for spreading base and hand tamping & edges in small areas
- Hand Tampers can be rented at equipment yards
- Plate Compactor can be rented to make sure you get a good compaction
- Water filled roller is a more affordable option to the Plate Compactor which will require more work. Also, you may need it in areas that are small or even sloping.

Materials Handling
- Bungee cords or rope for securing loads

The Artificial Grass roll will be heavy and will require the need of a helper. I recommend that you plan to have the roll delivered to a Staging area where it can be unrolled and cut into your smaller pieces that can then be moved into the Pattern.

EQUIPMENT AND TOOLS

Turf Cutting—Commercial Quality Knives and Blades (Make sure you select a blade and knife set that is easily changeable

Infilling
- Drop spreaders: I recommend (for small jobs) using the SCOTT®'s Brand Model 3000 (holds approx. 75 lbs of infill) or for larger areas, using the GrassHopper® Drop Spreader (holds approx. 200 lbs) or GANDY Corp.'s walk-behind or tow behind units.
- Installation and Grooming Rakes (poly-nylon)
- Grooming Hand tools (poly-nylon) (2 to 4)

Hand Tools
- Small Hand Shovel – used to clear and clean around pipes and tight edges
- Hammers
- Pliers (various sizes and shapes)
- Sledge Hammer (medium to large)
- Rubber Mallets
- Cement Chisel for hard edge finishing
- Straight Edge for measuring

Be sure and keep yourself safe by using these items —
- Rubberized and leather gloves
- Back Braces
- Knee Guards

Site Clean Up
- Water hose (100 ft) and Nozzle with variable heads
- Brooms (one soft bristle and one hard bristle)
- Small hand broom for rocks, edges, etc
- Shop vacuum
- Leaf blower (for clean up of organic materials and job site areas)

Misc. Tools
- Several small and large tarps
- Several small containers for used blades and small buckets for hand-filling, small tools and job materials
- Large Magnet to help scout for any nails or materials in the turf
- Carpet Kicker (optional) Very useful for helping turf   to lay snug while initially laying it out

Now you will need some supplies

- Benderboard and Stakes (100% Plastic): You will buy enough for the linear footage of all your hard edges. You should expect about $1.80 per foot and a stake every 3 feet for about .75 each
- You want to get some boxes of 5" Nails and some 6" Staples
- Several small and large tarps
- Several small containers for used blades and small buckets for hand-filling, small tools and job materials

Intentionally Left Blank

Step 3

Prepare The Site For Installation

In order to be ready to install your Artificial Grass you will need to prepare the site. This means that you will need to remove any natural sod, soil, problem concrete, asphalt or other existing materials that could impede a proper installation. You will be removing any surfaces down 3 to 4 inches below your final grade. Also, you will want to take into consideration the final grade (angle or slope for draining) of the project area.

TIP: Don't be tempted to rush through this stage.   A major reason that Artificial Grass Projects fail is that if you do not do a thorough job in this phase, you can have trouble with "Grade Failure." This means you will have parts of your new lawn where the ground sinks and creates loose wrinkles .

You will want be careful to complete each step just as I outline. Do not hurry or skip steps. Preparing your area is key to having a successful installation. In this stage you will be-
•Removing the Top Soil or existing Natural Grass
•Re-direct, Remove, or Cap off irrigation and <u>thoroughly test</u>
•Assure proper drainage system in the area
•Outlining the Artificial Grass (AG) area with your (2x2) Bend-a-Board
•Laying down your Base or Hard surface that your Artificial Grass will lay on.
•Re-grading and Smoothing as necessary and Compacting the Surface

•Cleaning up the Pattern Area and Bend-a-Boards of excess Base materials
 TIP: Irrigation Lines need to be tested for leaks before and after you seal them off. If you end up with leaks after your project is over than these leaks could ruin your whole project. Be careful and thorough with this step. Engage a professional if you do not feel sure about this step.

Remove the Top Soil or Sod:

You will want to take out and remove 3 inches of Top Soil in preparation for laying your Artificial Grass. You can do this by using shovels and Pick Axes if the soil is hard and rocky.

In order to save a great deal of time; you should rent a Sod Cutter as described in on Page 33. If you have a large Pattern (Project Area), the quickest way to remove the Sod is to go to your local Garden Center and rent a Sod Cutter. This machine will be well worth the rental amount for a day.

One way you can save time and effort in this step is to see if there are areas on your property that could accommodate the extra dirt from underneath your Sod or Grass. This will limit the amount of soil you will need to haul away.

Where you have Natural Grass or Sod you will want to remove all the grass <u>and its root system</u>. Remember, your new Artificial Grass will percolate (drain) water down into this "Native Soil" area. This "Native Soil" or original soils 3 to 4 inches below your Pattern can have elements that have a tendency to grow weeds underneath your new Artificial Grass installation. By being careful to remove all the roots and soil under those roots you will be preventing this problem.

Also, the Base or Rock layer that you will be applying in the next step may also have these elements that would produce weeds over time. Some instructions may coach you to install a Weed Barrier underneath your Base. My recommendation is to install any Weed Barrier after you have added your Base layer. Also, the Weed Barrier is a good Seaming Surface and provides insulation against any agitation of the Artificial Grass backing on your Base.

Try to leave smaller rocks you find while you are excavating. Removing them will cause you to need to purchase more base to refill in your Pattern area. These small rocks work well in your project area for proper drainage and getting a good compaction.

Re-direct, Remove, or Cap-off Irrigation Lines:

Now you will deal with any existing irrigation watering lines. You do not want any water to be leaking or draining into your Pattern Areas and will need to redirect, remove, or cap-off any irrigation lines. After you have modified the Irrigation then you will want to turn on the irrigation and check to make sure there is no water flowing into your pattern; since it can cause erosion of your compacted base. Take the proper time or get a landscape professional involved to make sure you accomplish this step.

Drainage System

If you are installing Artificial Grass on an area where there was Natural Grass previously then a proper drainage system may already be in place. Artificial Grass is very effective at allowing water to drain vertically into the soil like Natural Grass. Most of the time you will not need to be concerned since the current drainage system would accommodate your Artificial Grass installation as well. If the Natural Grass area had a lot of mold issues; then there may be drainage issues. With the area excavated, now would be an excellent chance to address drainage for the area.

If you are installing Artificial Grass in an area where there is no previous landscape or just cement than you will need to consider water drainage. The key is to slope the ground or install drainage systems to allow water to flow and not pool or gather around the foundations of structures. I would consult a landscape professional or even get the information from your local home improvement store about what would be effective and appropriate for the area.

PREPARE THE SITE FOR INSTALLATION

Install your Bend-a-Board in any Hard Edge areas:

There are many other installation procedures you will find that do not use this technique of using Bend-a-Board on Hard Edges. In my years of installing I have learned that this is a key difference between the long term durability and professional appearance of my installations.

Every area where there are hard edges on you Pattern, your will want to lay out your Bend-a-Board. This material will give you a place to anchor down and tuck your Artificial Turf. Your goal is to get the Bend-a-Board flush against the edge. Stake Bend-a-Board into place with grass stakes every 3 feet for straight edges. As you can see in illustrations below, you can also use Bend-a-Board with curved edges.

You will find the 100% Plastic Bend-a-board is extremely flexible and you will be able to use it on most curves. However, for tight curved edges, cut the Bend-a-Board with 45 degree angles slits every few inches depending upon how curved the edge is. Only if your curve is exceptionally sharp; use a saw to make these slit cuts. (Lay the slits away from the edge. You will also want to Stake every 2 feet for a curved edge.

Deposit your Base:

Now you are ready to create your hard Base surface that will be the foundation for your Artificial Grass. Contact your local Construction Materials Yard and have your base soil delivered to your home. The vendor you deal with will be able to advise you of quantities. As described in Chapter 2, you will need to tell them the Square Feet of the Pattern Area and that you are looking to have 3 inches of either Decomposed Granite or Concrete Miscellaneous Base.

TIP: If you notice that there are areas of the Pattern where you excavated more than 3 inches of Native Soil because of roots or larger rocks then you will want to plan for some extra Base to fill in that part of the Pattern. What you can do is just make an estimate of the square footage of those areas and order an additional inch of Base for that many square feet of the Pattern. It is more expensive to order a 2nd delivery than to have some extra Base.

Using a Wheel barrel you can dump your Base into the Pattern. Start with a back area that will allow you to lay out the base and not need to re-walk in that area after you have prepared it. Using the flat side of a leveling rake and a shovel you will spread the Base so that you are creating flat areas. One good leveling technique for flattening out areas is to take a 2x2 Wood board and slide along the surface and push excess base to other areas.

You will frequently need to be measuring and making sure you are creating a level grade before you begin to compact.

Compact Your Soil:

Once, you have a flat area in your Pattern you will want to water the area to eliminate dust. After the area has dried a bit you will now be ready to compact the Base. Start using either or both of the Compactors that were described in Section 2. If you have a small Pattern, then you can compact by using a Hand tamp. You want to create as flat and hard a surface as possible. As you are compacting you may need to keep moistening the soil to decrease dust. You need to keep lightly dampening the surface and compacting it until your surface starts to have a hard solid look. Sometimes it can look like wet cement.

Keep checking the grading (level of your Base) and make sure that you are leaving about an inch below your adjacent slab or sidewalk to lay your Artificial Grass. Your final grade needs to be almost level with existing elements such as walkways, driveways or patios. So allow adequate excavation and estimate the amount of Aggregate base you will use to raise the base to 1 inch below the final grade of the Hard Edge. You will want the turf of your Artificial Grass to extend above the grade so that it has that "look and feel" of Natural Grass.

You will want to use a Hand Tamp and do some extra compacting all around the edges. The Edges of your Pattern will be important in anchoring down your Artificial Grass and it is extremely important that the compaction be very firm.

Clean Areas around Bend-a-Board:

As a final step of Preparation you will want to clean all areas of excess soil. This is an important step that is often overlooked. You do not want any dirt or muddiness to get on top of the grass; or you will be creating extra work in the following stages. Brush any soil off of Bend-a-Board also. Use a flat 2x4 board to scrape off any soil that touches the upper ¼ inch of Bend-a-Board.

Make sure your drainage issues are resolved and checked. You may want to use a drainage Strip if there are large puddles.

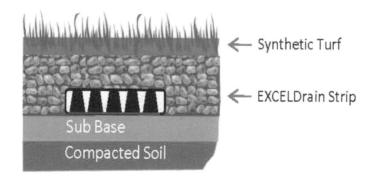

So with your Pattern/Project Area smooth, firm and compacted; and your irrigation and drainage issues resolved; and your Pattern and Bend-a-Board cleaned up; now you are ready to start laying your Artificial Grass.

Step 4

Install Your Artificial Grass and Lay Your In-Fill

Install Weed Barrier

You are now just a step away from cutting out your Artificial Grass sections and laying them out into your Pattern. Before you start this step you will want to roll out and nail down a durable Weed Barrier material on top of the Base.

As I stated before, some installation instructions do not specify a Weed Barrier or they instruct you to lay this Barrier or Fabric under the Base.

Roll out strips over your pattern and overlap them a few inches. You will want to nail down your Weed Barrier strips every few feet on both sides of the strip. Cut the Weed Barrier at the edges of your Pattern.

Cut your Artificial Grass Section

Now you will unroll your Artificial Grass and measure out and cut your first section that you are going to put into the Pattern. Using your design drawing cut your largest section off the roll.

1. Unroll the turf out to an approximate length you will be cutting.
2. Take measurements from the end of the roll and mark the back of the turf. Remember to give yourself an extra few inches on the cuts.

```
┌────────────────────────┐
│X--X----X---X----X      │
│                        │
│                        │
└────────────────────────┘
```

3. Now you can draw a straight line by connecting the marks you have made. You want the cuts to be very straight so   that seams will look great.

Another option is to purchase a "Chalk Line" for measuring.

INSTALL YOUR ARTIFICIAL GRASS AND LAY YOUR IN-FILL

After cutting the turf in a straight line, <u>ALWAYS</u> from the backing side; you can roll up that section and carry it to the area and lay the section onto the Area. Overlap your borders by an inch or so.

You will want to hammer in 5 inch nails along one of the edges about every 3 feet. Then you will want move along the surface of the turf and make sure that the turf is rolling out and becoming snug to the ground. Since the turf has been in a roll, you will need smooth it tightly into lying snug to the Weed barrier. Borrowing from the Carpet Industry; a Carpet Kicker is a good tool for this effort. You will not want to begin stapling, seaming or anchoring down the turf until it is lying very flat and snug.

A good technique to use is to continue hammering in 5" nails into the turf as you are spreading as illustrated. Now with the Artificial Grass spread out and overlapping the edges of the Pattern you will start going along those edges and nailing the Artificial Grass about 1 inch from the Hard or Soft Edge. Do not worry about the turf overlapping the Bend-a-Board since you are going to be tucking that portion between the Hard Edge and Bend-a-Board as a final step after the Artificial Grass surface is seamed and securely anchored down on the other edges.

Trim edges of padding with utility knife up to the edge of the Bend-a-Board. This means you will turn over the Artificial Grass and cut on the backing as you did when you cut it from the roll originally. Remember to allow about an inch of overlap over the Bend-a-Board Hard Edges.

INSTALL YOUR ARTIFICIAL GRASS AND LAY YOUR IN-FILL

 As you are going along the Edges make sure and keep using the Carpet Kicker to assure that the Artificial Turf is laying flat and tight on your Weed Barrier and Base. This will assure that you are not creating any wrinkles in your lawn.

As you start to get your edges snug you will start hammering in a nail along those edges about 6 inches on center. As your turf section is stretched and snug keep nailing rows of nails until you get to the side that will be seamed.

Do not nail down any rows of turf areas until after you have laid the turf around trees or other landscape objects. If you create hole in your pattern around a tree then you will want to staple and nail all the way around that hole so the Artificial turf section will stay snug on the edges. There is the option to use Adhesives or Glue in place of nails.

 When you lay out your second section you will want make sure that the grass pattern (direction the grass is facing) is in the same direction.

<u>Here is an important part</u>. Many installation instructions do not have this important step. You are going to eventually lay the straight edge section (the part that lines up with the Artificial Grass section you already laid) with a gap about 1/8th of an inch. I will cover this in detail in the Seaming section. For the moment, make sure there is a very small amount of overlap along the sides of the sections that will be seamed. Also, be sure that those sides are cut very straight so that they can be seamed to perfection.

You will keep laying the sections into the Pattern and snugging them and anchoring them as already described before. You will want to do the seaming on each section prior to doing the next section of Artificial Grass. When you encounter trees or other landscape items like Rock or Stepping Stones you will be cutting into the Artificial Grass and creating what ever desired borders.

Seaming

Seaming is a very important part of making your new Artificial Grass Lawn look natural and professionally installed. With the use of my instruction and some practice and patience you can be assured that your seams will not be seen in your new Artificial Grass lawn. Pay close attention and follow these steps to create unnoticeable seams:

Be sure that the edge has been removed to the first stitch row as seen in the illustration.

Line up two pieces of grass with about 1/8 inch gap between the 2 pieces of grass. The gap is necessary to keep the blades from piling up on each other.

Nail the two pieces down at the seam about 8 inches away from the seam edges. The nails should be about every foot. This will help make sure that the seam will lay flat with that 1/8 gap.

Now drive a nail on each side of the two sections at the seam as shown. Nail down approximately every foot along the seam.

As a final step, use the Staples and drive the leg of the staple on each side of the seam 6 inches between staples. Nail down Staples well with hammer so they do not create gaps in turf.

Alternative Seaming: If you are going to be seaming in an area where there will be kids playing; you can use another seaming technique. Follow the same instructions about creating the 1/8th gap. Instead of nails; pull back the turf and spread an adhesive about a foot wide and press the backing of the two sides down on the adhesive. You will then  weight down the seam and let them stand as directed by the instructions for the adhesive.

 Securing your Hard Edges:

Once your seams are done properly you are now ready to finish off the Hard Edges of that section of Artificial Grass.

Trim surplus grass about 1 inch from the perimeter of the edge. Use hammer and 2 inch chisel to tuck the surplus edge of the grass between the Bend-a-Board and the wall/edge as shown in the illustration.

TIP: If it is hard to get between the Hard Edge and Bend-a-Board you can use the head of your 5" Nails and Hammer to create a space for your Chisel or Wedge Tool.

Remove all excess Artificial Grass from area

INSTALL YOUR ARTIFICIAL GRASS AND LAY YOUR IN-FILL

Laying down your In-Fill:

Now you are going to lay down your In-Fill on your Artificial Grass. There may be a temptation to hurry through this step of Infilling; that would be a mistake. The key to infilling is patience and details. This important step will:

1) Perk up the blades and helps the first layer of infill to go down deep into the Artificial Grass. This will give your new lawn that full and natural look;
2) Anchor and weigh down the Artificial Turf to the ground and stop any horizontal slipping;
3) Cover over installation nails and staples while creating a nice bounce and softness to the texture of the grass; and
4) Allow you to customize a special layer in the grass for special applications like Putting Greens and Pet Areas. Pet areas will need in-fill that accommodates frequent pet urine and waste cleaning.

TIP: There is a product called Ziolite that can be spread in the Base under the turf of the Pet areas that will help minimize smells.

The process of laying down your Infill is systematically putting a layer of crumb rubber or round sand as an even layer over your Artificial Grass turf. Before you begin to spread any Infill into the Artificial Grass areas you will take a nice heavy duty brush (Shown in Illustration) and brush against the grain of the turf blades. You will see how the blades will start to stand up in those areas.

Now you will take a Drop or Sand Spreader filled with your In-fill and you will walk it over all the areas of a section of the Artificial Grass.

The plan will be to spread approximately 2 pounds of In-fill into every Square Foot of Artificial Grass. You will want to evenly spread a portion of this In-Fill on a section. Start in an obvious point where you can walk the area in a consistent pattern. DO NOT OVERLAP your efforts - this will create overly In-Filled lines throughout the finish. To assure you distribute Infill evenly, apply it in stages.

Use a Drop Spreader and evenly apply a portion of your Infill to an area. Take your brush once again and brush this layer into the turf. Now you will do a 2nd and 3rd application across each area so that the Infill has a chance to settle at the bottom layer of your grass.

Walk around the outer edges of the site to check for variances in color; lower spots will look lighter because the blade will be lying lower/flatter than properly filled surface areas. Dress lower areas by hand using a flat shovel and infill. Keep brushing Infill into surfaces, evenly.

INSTALL YOUR ARTIFICIAL GRASS AND LAY YOUR IN-FILL

IMPORTANT: Many other installation videos will use shovels or even hands and just randomly toss the In-fill around the area. In my opinion, this is not a good method and will not result in the best look. You will be creating patches of your Artificial Grass lawn where the In-fill will be missed. Those areas in time will look matted and flat. If a job is worth doing; it is worth doing right.

Some Key Tips for Infilling: If you observe these tips then you should not have any Over-filled areas to condition or re-work.

- Keep your infill materials DRY and CLEAN
- Clean all the site's surfaces of dirt, base and cut blades before you begin infilling. A good Shop Vacuum will be useful for this task.
- Clean Drop Spreader by clearing the infill residue with air pressure
- Use a Rolling Magnet or go over site very carefully looking for nails or staples.

After you have completely spread the In-Fill you will want to water the Artificial Grass areas and allow the water to move any remaining In-Fill down to the base layer.

Now you are almost completed with your Artificial Grass installation job and ready to begin enjoying your new lawn.

Take your heavy Duty Brush and do a final brushing and be looking out for loose debris in the Artificial Grass (nails, staples, AG fragments etc.)

Store or Return all your tools and equipment. Carefully package and store any extra Artificial Grass and Supplies. You will want to know where these supplies are if any repairs are necessary in the future.

Take a rolling magnet and carefully move it over your Pattern/Project Area and do a final search for any loose nails or staples.

 Using a high pressure hose, do a nice washing down of any dirt and dust of the Project around your Pattern Area. Now will be a great time to return all your Outdoor Furniture and Landscaping objects to their places. Be sure and take your "After" picture so you will be able to see what an amazing difference your new Artificial Grass lawn has made.

Congratulations on your successful installation. As I mentioned before, I would look forward to seeing your BEFORE and AFTER pictures and also serving as your "coach" by answering any questions you may have during your project.

As you now know, your new Artificial Grass Lawn does not have many of the maintenance issues that Natural Lawns have. In this next section I want to tell you what minimal maintenance there will be for you.

MAINTAINING YOUR NEW ARTIFICIAL GRASS LAWN

Maintenance for your new AG Lawn

You will want to rake or carpet brush your Artificial Grass lawn every few months. It helps to revitalize the pile (InFill), and bring small foreign objects to the surface. It will help to redistribute and "fluff" the upper surfaces.

Never use metal bristles or tools on the surfaces—they may break or shred the blades, creating weakness or causing damage to the surfaces. You can use a leaf blower to keep the leaves off your lawn.

Disinfecting your Artificial Grass every month. This can be accomplished in several ways.

- Turf Disinfectant – there are several enzymatic cleansers available. They are environmentally friendly and I highly recommend this process.
- Vinegar and Water wash – with a hose attachment or a pump sprayer, spray solution onto turf.
- Bleach Wash – diluted bleach will not discolor the turf. You can apply one tablespoon (20:1) of bleach per gallon of water.

Just like a Natural Grass lawn, animal droppings need to be picked up regularly and disinfecting will be a weekly process. Vinegar and enzyme cleaners are very effective against the smells animals can create. For animal feces and urine, use 1 gallon per 500 square feet of area and completely saturate the blades and infill. Rinsing the area within a few hours can help distribute these products deep into the surfaces. If you are experiencing odors, treat the area more regularly.

Trees and foliage that drop flowers, seeds or fruit upon the surfaces will require more attention. Most saps, fruit decomposition and organic droppings can be removed easily by spraying with vinegar and rinsing with a gentle shower of water, to dilute the sugars and wash them away.

Every year you should plan on doing a Rejuvenation Service. The deeper the Infill, the longer it will last. Sloped areas may also experience loss of infill than a flat surface. Upper level materials tend to be exposed to heavier traffic, UV and weather. A Rejuvenation Service will vacuum out layers of Infill and power brush with new In-fill. This will help recapture almost all of the original feel of the area.

Some cautions for keeping your new Artificial Grass Lawn looking great. Avoid allowing pure Alcohol or products with Alcohol on your lawn. Also, high heels will poke holes in the surface. Most woman take their high heels off before walking on Natural grass anyways. Finally, don't let any hot substances like burning coals from a barbecue near your Artificial Lawn.

You will spend some time and effort keeping your new Artificial Grass lawn fresh and clean. Compared with the maintenance involved with your old Natural Grass lawn you will enjoy all the time you have reclaimed.

Part 2

Launch Your Successful Artificial Grass Installing Business

Intentionally Left Blank

LAUNCH YOUR ARTIFICIAL GRASS INSTALLING BUSINESS

Starting your own business is not just about having a dream. There are real steps to ensure your business a successful start. So what are all of the things you should consider when launching your new business? In this section I will unveil a strong blueprint that will help you get past the learning curve that comes with any business.

According to business experts the real difficult issues that every business owner can face is that they are newly entering a market, having to establish supplier relations, keep initial cash flow and expenses under control, while training employees. To coordinate all these facets and start them simultaneously is a tremendous job. I was able to navigate these phases and I  have the experience and management background to help you be successful.

Quick word about business plans. Entrepreneurship researchers have studied how much better those who started businesses with a formal, written plan did than those who didn't. What they found out was that entrepreneurs who began with formal plans had no greater success than those who started without them. That being said, the real surprise is that they found that writing a plan greatly increased the chances; **by 250%,** that a person would actually go into business.

So don't let planning get in the way of taking the actions necessary to launch your business. I certainly am not claiming to be a business expert; however, I have my experience to give you from the years I have built my businesses. There are some critical pieces you will need to get your plan together and have a successful launch.

This Part of the book will be useful in giving you the information you need to take action on. I will not speak to business fundamentals, as much as Artificial Grass Installation business fundamentals. You can find key areas to focus on in the coming chapters and be able to do some careful planning.

As a business owner, you will need a plan to avoid pitfalls, to achieve your goals and to build a profitable business.

So here are the major tasks ahead of you to be successful:
1) You will need a practical plan with a solid foundation;
2) Also, you will need the dedication and willingness to sacrifice to reach your goal;
3) You will need to get the technical skills involved in Artificial Grass Installation;
4) You will need basic knowledge of management, finance, record keeping and market analysis.

Make a commitment to master these skills and disciplines; being committed gives you a great edge on becoming successful. If over time you will manage and develop these key areas of your new business; you can be very confident in your success. Always be willing to listen to good ideas about these areas:

Marketing Programs and Partners	Designing and Estimating Projects
Referral Selling	Scheduling the Projects
Ordering Materials and Supplies	Installing the Projects
Making Corrections	Working Trade Shows
Public Relations	Hiring and Training
Bill Paying and Collections	Record Keeping
Legal compliance	Strategic Planning
Production Reporting	Communications and Systems

I decided to look at these key areas by dividing them up into four chapters. First I will talk about your initial setting up of the business. Then I will deal with Marketing and Attracting your clients. Estimating and Presenting the project to these clients will be next. Finally, I will talk about Implementing the project and the operations part of your business.

Before we get going; I want to discuss one more important idea.

LAUNCH YOUR ARTIFICIAL GRASS INSTALLING BUSINESS

Are you an ideal person for the Artificial Grass Installation Business ?

Are you a good match for this business? You will be your most important employee. Take an important moment and appraise your strengths and your weaknesses. Business experts believe these characteristics seem to distinguish the person who starts their own new business from the person who works for someone else.

Strong Opinions and Attitudes: If you are going to risk your money and time in your own business you must have a strong feeling that you will be successful.

Need to Achieve: If you want to open your own business, you are likely to have a strong "Need for Achievement". This "Need for Achievement" is a another word for motivation and is usually an important factor in success.

Risk Taker: When a person starts and manages his own business they do not always see risks; they see only factors that they can control to their advantage. We want to delve into those factors you can control.

Other Important Traits: Drive, thinking ability, competence in human relations, and communications skills.

For installing Artificial Grass you should enjoy working outdoors. Have a real drive to help homeowners, maintenance managers, athletic directors, golfers. For myself, I liked to see the faces on my customer and even the kids when they first see their new Artificial Grass lawn.

I want to give you some background about the Artificial Grass Industry and look at the bright future ahead for the industry.

Intentionally Left Blank

Chapter 1

The Artificial Grass Business

 The Artificial Grass market has been consistently strong the past ten years. The market has grown 20% for the last 5 years, increasing the landscape and leisure sports markets to 35-40% of the market.

The Artificial Grass market is currently growing at 20 percent annually, according to industry statistics. That number is expected to hold, if not grow, as an increasing number of communities and water districts nationwide restrict outdoor water use and more homeowners seek more environmentally friendly ways to enjoy outdoor landscaping without pesticides, fertilizers or expensive upkeep.

It is projected that this part of the market will increase to include any kind of lawn or "landscape" element including slopes, erosion control, outdoor amphitheaters, indoor atriums, theater, films, store front or window treatments. Other emerging markets include show booths, outdoor dining areas, parks, pet play areas, daycare centers, pet kennels, senior centers, bocce ball or lawn bowling. Also, there are some applications gaining popularity using Artificial Grass for grey-water management, erosion and dust-control; and even creating Green Roofs!

The synthetic grass industry is going from strength to strength with a healthy increase in the number of people who are converting their natural grass lawns to new synthetic grass lawns. The moves have been prompted by a number of factors such as areas that are in drought and are experiencing heightened water restrictions that have made it difficult to keep a lawn alive.

Artificial grass has come a long way in terms of the technological enhancements. Improvements are being made to ensure the grass is lead-free and safe to use and will continue to be safe as it ages. A lot of work is also being put into the appearance of residential synthetic grass to ensure that it looks as near in appearance as natural grass as possible. These days it is very difficult to tell that the lush green lawn that you are admiring is actually fake grass.

THE ARTIFICIAL GRASS BUSINESS

A similar but separate industry is the synthetic turf industry that supplies and installs artificial turf surfaces for sporting arenas, playgrounds, schools and other commercial locations. Like the residential synthetic grass manufacturers, the makers of this turf have made huge advancements in the quality and reliability of their products. Factors such as the safety of the athletes  using it and the effect the surface has on the way each sport is played on it have been taken into careful consideration in the past and will continue to be significant factors in the future.

In areas where there is high rainfall are also benefited by Artificial Grass. In fact, most Artificial Grass in the past years have been installed in these states. Lawns with too much waterfall need special maintenance. These lawns can have drainage issues that will cause pools and swamping and resulting issues with mold. Also, these high rainfall areas still have issues with chemicals and fertilizers that are used on lawns being absorbed into the water table and draining into storm drains and water systems.

The Future for Artificial Grass: Growing consciousness about conserving the earth's water resources and stemming the tide of water pollution will keep the Artificial Grass industry relevant. Estimates are that 36 states will experience water shortages in the next 5 years. Legislation and restrict water use for irrigation will become frequent along with rebates to install Artificial Grass lawns. Artificial grass is a perfect solution.

Homeowner Associations use to be able to restrict Artificial Turf. However, that tide is changing. In California, legislation was enacted forbidding Homeowner Associations from restricting Artificial Grass installations.

The industry is still young with many innovations yet to come. Artificial grass is a very attractive option and in most of the country a very small percentage of prospects have yet to replace their natural landscapes with Artificial Grass.

Intentionally Left Blank

Chapter 2

Setting Up Your Artificial Grass Business

In this section I want to give you a plan for getting your Artificial Grass Installation business prepared to launch. There will be eight areas that you will need to give your attention to as you start servicing your new customers. Each of these areas is important to consider no matter what size operation you are planning. If you are going to grow your business starting with just yourself and running the business out of your home, then some of these tips will be useful as you are launching your expansion.

The first question you want to answer is: How much money will I need to launch my business? This question will be answered after these decisions are made.

We are going to look at the following areas:

- Facilities and Office Location
- Selecting Artificial Grass Supplier and other supply Vendors
- Red Tape: Licenses, Bonding and Insurance
- Tools and Equipment
- Administration and Organizing your Recordkeeping
- Hiring your first employees
- Training Issues

Facilities and Office Location

Homebased Location: If you decide to launch your business from your home then you will want to consider some of these ideas. Your primary markets will be the homeowners and businesses close to your home area. You will still want to create a professional image. Be sure and look closely at the Marketing Section in the next Chapter. You will want to invest in a quality website and voicemail service.

On your business cards you may want to find a local postal box service that can give you an address on a main street. Your advantage will be that you are glad to meet your prospect at their place and without the higher overhead you can be more competitive (not cheap) with your pricing. You will want to make sure and have magnetic signs or graphics on all your cars to market the business.

Facilities/Offices:

If you decide to get an office in a business center I would recommend that you look at these factors. You will not need a very large office space. Look to get an office that has street traffic or highway visibility. Ideally, you should look to see if there are locations near home improvement centers. If you secure these locations you will be able to put up some excellent signage that will attract curious prospects to stop in and inquire about Artificial Grass.

Another consideration is to choose a location where you will have easy access to a large supply store and a materials yard. Not only will you benefit from those businesses' marketing and foot traffic; but you will be able to conveniently pick up needed supplies. In the Artificial Grass industry you will not likely find too many competitors; but it is worth checking for their presence in your prospective locations.

With a office location you will want to post and keep office hours so that you can take advantage of walk-in prospects. Consider a location where there are a lot of high quality neighborhoods where owners will be able to find your office or you will be able to market for installations. This location factor will help with generating quality prospects and at the same time help as you grow and need quality staffing.

Be sure and put lighted signs in your windows and place visible signs that will make it easy for your business to be seen and easy to know what your business is about. This is why the name you choose is important to create that impression. I will give you some guidance about this in the Marketing Section coming up. Remember to put signage on any of your vehicles that are parked in front of the business location.

Besides having a place to store tools, equipment, and business  records; your office location should have an area of the office be a little area for a mini showroom of your grass samples and pictures showing finished projects that will help your prospect visualize what your service will do for them. Make sure and negotiate a lease where you will be able to make changes as you grow.

Training and On-Going Education: There are some resources in the Special Section at the back of the book about Industry Information that will help you to gain more skill and understanding about the Artificial Grass Industry. Also, you should always be ready to learn and get new insights by staying current with bulletins and trade information that you can have sent to you.

Artificial Grass is heavy and expensive to ship. Unless you are selecting from discontinued or overstock turfs, your final price will often be a factor of how far your supplier or distributor was required to ship the Artificial Grass from. Make it a regular activity to explore these Artificial Grass selections that are specially priced. If you can, find a supplier that will agree to give you leads for jobs. Make sure they have a strong internet presence with a well-marketed website.

For example, you may be an installer in Florida who chooses a supplier of Artificial Grass locally. That supplier may be having their Artificial Grass shipping from a large manufacturer in Texas. If you select a supplier or distributor that will supply from a manufacturer in Georgia you will have a great advantage on price because of the shipping factor.

Another key factor in choosing a supplier that is very well-capitalized so they stock turf you need in the quantities you need for your installations. There are two key advantages to this strategy. Once you sell a job you don't want to have to be waiting for the supplier to get your shipment. Also, on a larger job, your supplier will need to be able to supply a same Die Lot or Same Run turf product for you. Similar to matching paint, this means that the whole order would be assured of having a matching hue and coloring.

To review, you need to align your business with large supplier or distributor; since they will be buying at the largest volumes and may be able to create a pricing advantage for your customers. Even if your larger supplier purchases from a manufacturer that is farther away; they still may buy at a much larger volume that could overcome that factor. Still, you need to be aware that many suppliers claim they are a manufacturer; and they may be getting their turf from a part of the country that is not as competitive because of shipping.

You may decide to distribute your Artificial Grass purchases among many suppliers to gain more favorable prices and promotional material. Another strategy is to concentrate your grass purchases among a single supplier to develop a stronger relationship. Which ever strategy you use; you now understand the various issues involved so that you can make the right approach with suppliers as you grow your volume. Also, you can work as an advocate to get the right pricing and types of varieties that your customers are looking to install. It is important for you to keep tabs on developments in the industry as you manage your supplier relationships. Be sure and take time to look at the websites of Manufacturers and Suppliers shown in Special Section.

Choosing Your Artificial Grass Types

You will want to look at as many types of Artificial Grass as you can and make decisions about the ones you will promote. I always choose lead-free turfs and ask for the supplier to provide certification. The main reason your clients will choose a certain type will be the "look and feel" of the turf. There will always be budget issues; but the appeal and aesthetics of the Artificial turf selections will be the main deciding factor. This is a good reason to stay current with what new options you can offer your client. I have seen how so many installers will stay with a certain type and soon all the installers are selling the same choices and the decision is reduced to just the price.

What I think is wise is to be presenting three choices to the customer. Have an "Economical" option. This could be a 1-1/4 inch 45 to 50 ounce turf. Then present a "Better" option. You could offer a 1-1/2 inch 64 to 60 ounce Multi–Colored option. Finally, have a "Best" option. This could be a 2 inch 80 ounce Dual Filament Multi-Colored turf. When the client feels the differences they will appreciate you helping them make the best choice.

Economical/Good

Better Option

Best Option

Something to consider is your location in the country. For instance, on the East Coast, most of the natural lawns are a darker green than here in California or in Florida. Here in California lawns are lighter with brown thatch. So you will want to tailor your selections to create that natural look.

The Pile Height of the Yarn is a factor to pay attention to. The Pile Height and Face Weight will cause a difference in pricing. Generally speaking, pricing will increase based on how much material (ie. Yarn), processing time, and steps are necessary for the manufacturers. For your "Best" option you will want to look at the Multi-Directional Yarns since they look and feel even more like natural grass. You will be able to notice the differences between Ridged and Softness and so will your clients.

As I stated earlier, shipping cost is an important factor in pricing. However, I have also found that most of the time the more expensive turf will often be a more durable product; so remind your customer of this.

Sometimes your client may be concerned about creating a very resilient "fall zone" where children are playing. You will want to have a high face weight turf for these occasions; however, this option would not be a common choice.

For your Putting Green clients you will want to show a 3/4 or 1/2 inch Nylon with some variation of colors. At times they may want to have a putting green that has an outlined "fringe" or a 2nd outline "rough" section.

Red Tape and Legalities: Licenses, Bonding and Insurance

The Artificial Grass industry is regulated differently in all the various states. You will need to contact your state and local agencies to find the exact details for launching your business. For instance, in California, you need to have very specific Contracting Licenses and other states will not require any licensing. I found the Contractor test to be very easy to test for. If your state does require licensing; search online for helpful agencies that can provide testing preparation so you will successfully acquire your licenses.

Part of licensing will give you the necessary information you need about required bonding and insurance. Do not be discouraged by these requirements, bonding is not expensive and it is a selling point for your professionalism. Some states will also define what are considered proper bids or proposed project and necessary design documents.

Also, you will want to check with your local city about business permitting. This will be necessary when you negotiate your business location.

Some Legal Issues to Pay Attention To:

Corporate Structure: There are so many good advisors to talk with so you can properly set up your new company structure to maximize your tax advantages.

Contracts and Business Forms: Standard contracts and invoices with your Company Logo and information will usually suffice for your new business. Be sure and get advice for peculiarities that must be observed in your Contracts and Agreements regarding your state and area. For instance, in California, one good practice is to have a Notice of Right to Lien on Invoices to help speed up any collection issues. Also, make sure you are protected from any liabilities with waivers against injury to large trees in the project areas.

Be sure and get a Resellers Permit: You will not need to pay Sales Tax on the items you are selling to your customers on your projects. What I did in my business was assigned a percentage of each project to supplies for the project and charged my client sales tax on that portion.

Some contractors want to avoid the tax issue with clients and will include the sales tax in their project cost and not itemize tax to their clients. They were advised that they are "saving" the cost of personal taxes on the additional profit margin. Make sure and get the best advice in this area.

Be sure to check with your state and federal regulations: Talk with competent advisors about regulations you may need to pay close attention to as a business in this industry. For instance, you may need to have regular Safety Meetings under the Department of Occupational Safety.

Tools and Equipment

 As you read in Part 1 on Installing there are tools and equipment that you will initially be able to rent for the installations you are doing. However, as you grow your business you will want to capitalize your business with equipment that you will be using very frequently. At the beginning you can maintain the Rental Yard relationships; however, in time you will want to purchase those machines and equipment. Especially since you can plan on growing to the point of having multiple work crews operating on the same day.

Since you will be doing multiple installs per week (or day), you will want to get the equipment that saves time and builds profits. For instance, instead of brushing with a Industrial Broom you should look at getting a Gas powered Power Brush. You can plan to invest in all the energy and time saving powered equipment and stop renting. This will help with your scheduling as well.

Record Keeping

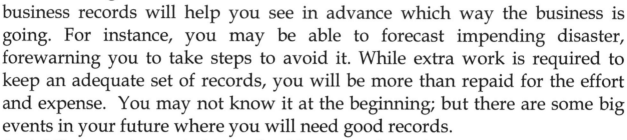

One essential element of business management is the keeping of adequate records. Virtually all studies show that business failures can be attributed to a combination of inadequate records and the owners failing to use what information was available to them. Good business records will help you see in advance which way the business is going. For instance, you may be able to forecast impending disaster, forewarning you to take steps to avoid it. While extra work is required to keep an adequate set of records, you will be more than repaid for the effort and expense. You may not know it at the beginning; but there are some big events in your future where you will need good records.

1. Adding a major capital item (buildings, trucks, etc)
2. Taking on an investment partner for expansion
3. Selling the business

If you are not prepared to keep adequate records - have someone keep them for you. You can start and grow with a system like Quick Books. But more importantly, you need them to run your business successfully and to increase your profits. With an adequate, yet simple, bookkeeping system you can answer such questions as:

- How much business am I doing?
- Which expenses appear to be too high?
- What is my gross and net profit margin?
- What is the status of my working capital?
- How much do I owe my suppliers?

Keep track of the trends in my receipts, expenses, profits, and net worth so you can see improvements in your financial situation or where best to spend your efforts.

- How do my assets compare with what I owe?
- What is the percentage of return on my investment?
- How many cents out of each dollar of sales are net profit?

Do your business a great favor by keeping this data in a detailed and orderly fashion and you will be able to answer these questions. Before you decide to maintain a record, answer these three questions:

1. How will this record be used?
2. How important is the information likely to be?
3. Is the information available elsewhere in an equally accessible form?

<u>Work up and Keep a budget</u> to help you determine just how much increase in profit is reasonably within your reach. The budget will answer some important questions:

- What sales will be needed to achieve my desired profit?
- What fixed expenses will be necessary to support each project?
- What variable expenses will be incurred?

 A budget enables you to set a goal and determine what to do in order to reach it. Compare your budget periodically with actual operations figures. Then, where discrepancies show up you can take corrective action before it is too late.

<u>Inventory</u>: One of the important records I discovered to be useful is the Die Lot and Roll Numbers of Artificial Grass that you purchase. If you have some issue with a warranty or repair later on you will be glad you kept the records. One method that works good for Inventory records is to have a sheet with the details on each roll purchased. Then you can have a row where you document anyone cutting off lengths or using up that turf in particular projects.

<u>Customer Management System</u>: Make sure to keep thorough records on your customers. You may want even use the same system to track prospects, referrals, vendors. As you develop your business have a process to capture this information. You will be able to use this valuable data to assure good follow-up service which will generate more projects.

Hiring your first employees

If your business will be large enough to require outside help, an important responsibility will be the selection and training of employees. You may start out with family members or business partners to help you; but as the business grows the time will come when you must select and train personnel.

To select the right employees determine beforehand what you want each one to do. As you do the different tasks of your business you can begin to develop Job Descriptions and a Handbook of Procedures. This will be very helpful as you start to bring on your first employees. Look for flexible employees who can shift from task to task as required.

Some sources of possible new employees are:

- Recommendations by friends, business acquaintances
- Employment agencies. Placement bureaus
- Help-wanted ads on the internet (Craig's List) or local newspapers.

Ask your questions carefully to find out about the applicant. References are a must, and should be checked. Try to verify that the information given to you. On your initial conversation and at the interview listen very closely for any comments that are made. Also, listen for what is not said; like missing details.

A well-selected employee is only a potential asset to your business. Whether or not he or she becomes a real asset depends upon your training. Allow

sufficient time for training. Give them time to learn and grow. Use projects as training opportunities and remember to follow up and see how they are reacting to their training.

Chapter 3

Marketing and Attracting Clients

MARKETING AND ATTRACTING CLIENTS

The most important of launching a successful installation business will be setting up your marketing plan that will be able to supply you with prospective clients. Even though there are many marketing avenues you can pursue that will help you get  your business out there; I want to spend this first section talking about the most vital marketing approach.

Setting up your Website and Referral Systems

In the Artificial Grass installing business your website will be the most important marketing tool you have in your arsenal. In general the public does not understand the value of Artificial Grass. Consequently they will be looking for reasons and information that will convince them that they should be investing in Artificial Grass. In the past years the Internet is the primary way that your prospects and clients will be finding the information they need.

Therefore, your website needs to be information rich. Also, your website needs to have a design that will allow your prospects to find the information you are offering and engage you in a sales consultation. You will want to offer a regular newsletter that will keep your business name in front of those who visit your website for information on Artificial Grass. This engaging is often called "converting."

So what are your steps to getting your Website launched and having a good Internet Presence? In this section I want to advise you on three critical steps:
1. Finding an experienced Web Designer
2. Getting your website found
3. Driving Traffic to your website

MARKETING AND ATTRACTING CLIENTS

Finding a Web Designer

Once you have talked with other business acquaintances and have some referrals on some possible web designers; you need to ask the developer if you can see some samples of their work before you arrange a meeting. Look at the website and see if you find their websites appealing and professional looking.

Arrange a meeting where you will get these questions answered.

Question 1. If you designed my website, how does my website get promoted in the search engines?
You are testing to see if they have a good understanding of web site promotion on the search engines.

Question 2. What design techniques would you use to make sure my website can be found?
They need to know about search words and how your website needs to be designed with search words that are common. Anyone can show you a website where it can be found using search words that are not a common searches or what are known as "competitive searches." Don't be easily fooled by this common trick of Web Designers who will show you Google hit lists of their website using searches that would not commonly be used by the general public.

Question 3. How long does it take before I start seeing traffic on my website?
You are testing for their understanding of the proper timeframes of your site being promoted in the Internet Searches. If the designer insinuates that it will be quick then you best take your business elsewhere. It can take several

months to see your website start managing traffic.

Getting your Website Found

Search Engine Optimization or SEO is a quickly changing and evolving part of the Internet. You do not have time to become your own SEO technician; just as many areas of business you can rely on others. I would like to introduce you to some key aspects that are unique for the Artificial Grass industry.

There are the "TOP 6" main Search Words for the Artificial Grass Industry which you will want to make sure your web designer uses:
1) Artificial Grass
2) Artificial Turf
3) Artificial Lawn
4) Synthetic Grass
5) Synthetic Turf
6) Synthetic Lawn

Also make sure that when a Internet user types in "Buy" with any of these 6 search words. There are many techniques associated with SEO (Search Engine Optimization) work and the pest practices are changing rapidly. It is important that your designer is staying current.

 TIP: It is important that your Web Designer knows how to uses these words richly throughout your site so that you will have the necessary advantage of being found by prospects.

Driving Traffic to Your Website

Search Engine Optimization will be your lowest cost method to find prospects and new customers using the internet. I would like to make sure you know about other important ways to harvest new prospects.

You should have your website advertised on every piece of paper that ever leaves your office. Yes, that means your invoices, emails, letterhead; absolutely everything.

Also, you will want to create a free offer or Report to give people a good reason to visit. Offers of interesting information or subscription to a useful free regular newsletter you can send are effective directions. You can send your subscribers regular information that involves water conservation or other interesting ideas that would be useful to homeowners.

I don't recommend this next method because of the financial risks. However, you can get traffic to your website by purchasing it. Besides looking for advertising sources locally where people can learn about your website; there are internet services that will set up websites and landing sites that will find leads for you. These services are known as "Pay-per-click." Although there are various pricing strategies; sources that I know in the Artificial Grass industry say that this will not likely be a useful avenue for you to explore. As

discussed earlier, many prospects are looking for information initially and these leads may end up costing as much as $6 per lead. That means that most of each $6 you spend would not result in a conversion or profitable sale.

MARKETING AND ATTRACTING CLIENTS

A final internet based marketing idea I want to acquaint you with is using a service that specializes in finding you leads in connection with their network of installers. There are distributors that are willing to put you on their website as a link for customers in your region of the company that visit distributors website. This is a great option if that distributor passes the test for being your best vendor option. You need to be able to endorse the Artificial Grass selections of that distributor and be getting the most profitable pricing.

WEB-BASED SOCIAL NETWORKING
The emergence of Facebook, Twitter, and YouTube for business use is a fascinating occurrence to be sure. These websites allow you to create a free business presence and attract possible consumers who traffic heavily in those mediums. Facebook is worth considering since it is the 2nd most widely visited website in the world. (2nd only to Google Search)

CALL OUT: Remember, your best "Advertising" will be the word-of-mouth created by doing great work and the referrals you get from customers.

Although, I admit that using Facebook or Twitter to contact your business, for the moment, does seem to belong to younger consumers; it would be useful to have your Web designer put the major links on your website and set up free accounts.

You can have each of these services alert you on your email if someone contacts you through their social networking media. There is information you can readily find on line for making business contacts with Facebook and Twitter. Once you have your website generating leads and searches you will be able to learn techniques and strategies that will use only 15 minutes a day generating interest in Artificial Grass and your business specifically with these avenues.

Other Marketing Channels you want Launch

Create quality marketing tools. Make a list of everything you're going to need each time you make contact with a prospective customer or client, including a stationery package, brochures and presentation tools. Just like your website, it is important to use very appealing and professionally produced materials. Get the right help from those who specialize in creating these promotional materials that will give your prospects and customers the right impression. TIP: Remember to advertise your website on every single paper that comes from your business.

TIP: Marketing Pieces: Many business have tried to promote AG with banners such as "$1.99/square foot." I would recommend that you promote the other benefits and talk more about return on investment. While you are doing research of your markets you should visit Artificial Grass Installer and Distributor websites and get ideas for good marketing brochures for your company.

Other Marketing Tools:

BUSINESS NAME/LOGO: As described above, your business name should tell prospects that you specialize in Artificial Grass and what area you will service will help also. The location in your name may be a common search word for local prospects looking on the Internet. Once you have settled on a name you should combine it with a high quality Logo. Your logo needs to create a good impression with your prospects and clients. Take some time and look at many logos that are impressive or invest in a designer that will provide a logo that is polished and has that professional appeal.

Uniforms: Take your Name/Logo and get it put on quality Embroidered apparel for you and your sales reps to wear to appointments or trade shows. Also, you should have a comfortable shirt made up for you and any work crew members to wear during installation jobs. This impression is  all part of your Marketing image and will pay in customers that will want to give you references to their friends and acquaintances.

Office Communications: When anyone calls your business, you have a chance to create a good Marketing image. It is important to make sure your company has a professionally sounding person to answer calls or a voice mail system that can give the caller a strong sense that your business is competent and capable to help them with their Artificial Grass interests.

You have just a few seconds to create that first impression. A friendly, inviting, and helpful attitude are some characteristics to project when answering your phones.

If you are going to only have voicemail initially, invest in a service that will handle multiple calls coming in. Busy signals give the wrong impression. Create an incoming call greeting that will leave the strong impression that you are not only glad they called, but that you will be getting their message and responding promptly. Make sure you can be alerted by text or pager when a call has been  received so you can be sure and be responsive. Believe me, responsiveness will distinguish you in your market.

Offer work samples: This is an excellent program for creating interest. Find restaurants or areas that have high traffic. You can use some of your left over remnants of Artificial Grass and install a lawn in a small area around the entrance. While customers are waiting for a table or reviewing the menu they will see your grass installation or message about the Artificial Grass. You could have a classy sign posted or maybe an insert in the  menu.   This message serves two purposes at the same time. First, it will tell the restaurants customers that the restaurant is concerned about water conservation. While this will help create a favorable impression you will be promoting your business as a source for them to learn more about the benefits of Artificial Grass.

Get on Bid Lists: Many cities have started to create initiatives and programs encouraging water conservation. Believe it or not, even in areas where water is abundant, the costs are climbing faster for water delivery than in water-scarce areas.   That means that you should find out about government bids for Artificial Grass in all the cities, counties, and government entities. Many of the utility companies and public colleges in your area are managed with open bid processes. Getting notification of potential jobs you can bid on is a very good use of your time and marketing resources.

 **Local Trade Shows, "Market Nights" or Fairs:**   Search and locate all your community calendars and find events where you can regularly set up a booth that can attract prospects and new customers.

Remember to focus on your best market niche. Your primary niche will be the many homeowners in all the surrounding cities you are servicing. You will want to regularly align your marketing efforts with events that are targeting homeowners. Many areas have expos and shows where they are showing home improvement ideas. Don't forget your hardware stores that may be having events where you may be able to create a co-marketing event.

Offer your help: You want to be known as a businessperson that is concerned for your community and willing to give back. One way that you can do that is to align your company with reputable community non-profit organizations. You can become apart of fundraising efforts and programs that benefit schools or disadvantaged segments. This will allow your business name to get into the hands of potential homeowners who will admire your concern and want to inquire about Artificial Grass. One way to effectively be known as a service-oriented business is to join up with some of the business groups.

Network with Business Groups: Find the quality business networking groups in your area to be active with. Whether it is the  Chamber of Commerce, Rotary Club, or Kiwanis, the key is to find a way to participate with the goals and service activities. Just showing up for networking events is not usually the best use of your time. In the course of helping with the outreach activities you will become known by the businesses in the organization and sales referrals will become common.

There is a group known as Business Networking International (BNI) that will often have many active chapters within your area. Your first visit allows you to watch the networking in action and see if that group would be a good investment of your time.

Create Press Releases or have some one do that and get them sent to local papers or radio news. Become a speaker that can discuss relevant information regarding cutting water use or helpful home improvement news. These topics can be useful for local media groups to feature.

Cross-promote/Co-Market with other businesses: While networking with other contractors and related home improvement specialties in your area you will notice that you are meeting with the same prospects. There are business services that you could promote while you are on sales opportunities. For instance a contractor that specializes in installing Ponds, Waterfalls, or Paving. Before you develop a Co-marketing relationship, make sure that you can count on their workmanship and customer service since you will referring them to your customers and prospects.

TIP: This is also an additional opportunity for extra website marketing. If your Co-marketing partners have websites than you will be able to drive additional traffic to your website by putting links to each other's websites.

Become the expert in your area: Local newspapers and radio/TV media are often looking for stories of interest to present to readers and listeners. As you learn more about your industry and Artificial Grass installation you will be able to write articles, or offer to be interviewed about the benefits of Artificial Grass. This will give you a chance to have your business promoted as a great resource for homeowners or businesses to learn about the benefits of installing Artificial Grass. You can continue to build your image as an expert as you tell viewers or readers about your website and offer your free newsletter.

Training seminar or share a seminar for home-improvement: As you become more confident with installing Artificial Grass you can become known as a trainer by offering to teach or tutor homeowners or contractors who want to learn to install. You can offer to demonstrate the techniques at a seminar or class and even offer to bill your services to come on site and help or train during an installation. The key is that you will be able to pick up additional sales opportunities and continue to be seen as the expert in your area.

Referral Marketing: To conclude this section on Marketing; I wanted to leave the best Marketing program for last. In case you did not read my Biography at the beginning of the book; this technique of Referral Marketing is a primary way that I believe I was able to experience the success I've had in the Artificial Grass installation business.

As the owner or CEO of your business you will be the face of your business. Your personality and skill will be reflected in the impressions and contacts that prospects make about your business. It is important for you to have a passion for the product and service you supply and to prove that passion everyday by making warm and personable contact with friends and acquaintances you have. Some keys with Referral Marketing are that you be sincere in wanting people to know about the Artificial Grass and the benefits and that you are wanting your friends to get the best installation and the best possible price.

This may mean that you will be using extra hours and going the extra mile and even giving wholesale pricing to your friends so that they can become part of your team of people that will refer their friends and acquaintances. This means that sometimes you will need to do installations where you are not very profitable as an investment in many other installation jobs where you will not need to work hard to get the installation contract.

As you start getting these referral sales and projects you will want to treat that new referred customer as a golden opportunity to have them join your referral team as well. This means that you will make sure that every installation project has your high standards and that you find something extra special to add to the project. A few ideas may be:
- Do a complimentary pressure-wash at the end of the job
- Surprise your customer by giving them some extra Artificial Grass for them to store in case there are repairs needed; or
- Include a complimentary "rejuvenation service" after 6 months.

Selecting Artificial Grass Suppliers and other Vendors

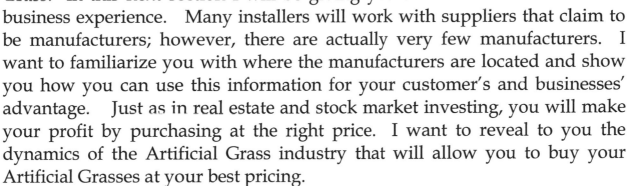

It is important that you find your best supplier for Artificial Grass. In this next section I will be giving you some critical business experience. Many installers will work with suppliers that claim to be manufacturers; however, there are actually very few manufacturers. I want to familiarize you with where the manufacturers are located and show you how you can use this information for your customer's and businesses' advantage. Just as in real estate and stock market investing, you will make your profit by purchasing at the right price. I want to reveal to you the dynamics of the Artificial Grass industry that will allow you to buy your Artificial Grasses at your best pricing.

In the Special Section there is a list of Manufacturers that each have companies that distribute the Artificial Grass. To become one of these distributors that can purchase direct, you need to be able to be purchasing large quantities of Artificial Grass every month. Of course, this is a function of your sales activities. As you grow your sales and installation volume you will be able to make alliances to purchase your Artificial Turf at even more favorable pricing.

For the moment, you need to recognize that the supplier you choose may be aligned with only certain distributors and those distributors may only have certain manufacturers that they purchase from. This creates two challenges. You may only have access to certain varieties of Artificial Grass and also the pricing and costs on the Artificial Turf will not be your best price.

You do not want to only be limited to the same types and varieties of Artificial Grass as other installers in your area. Try to carry selections that others in your area don't have. I even like to create brochures that show the products with my business branding. So take the time to explore various suppliers or distributors of certain Manufacturers. As you learn the different varieties of Artificial Grass you will be able to notice certain similarities.

In a very classy way, make sure they know these are gifts and added benefits that they choose your business. When you have finished the job and when you come back for their 6 month rejuvenation you can then ask  them for referrals.

Asking for Referrals:

The most effective way to get referrals is to start talking about them during the sales process. I will show you more about that in the next section on Estimating and Sales; just to say, when you are telling them about happy customers and reference accounts you will be preparing your prospect for the time you are going to be asking for referrals.

Here is a possible question to use for asking for referrals. You can adapt it so that it feels natural to you. You can ask,

"Are there any close friends or relatives; people you golf with; or regularly do business with that you think would like to know about your Artificial Grass installation?"

Notice that you are not just asking if they know someone; but rather suggesting some different groups of people that will stick out in their minds. Another good tip for Referral Marketing is that you can even ask people who are only asking about Artificial Grass and are not customers. This may happen at trade shows or during networking events.

You may want to soften the question about referrals by asking, "Would you be able to help me with something?" Many people are very responsive to this approach and are eager to help others. Take advantage and leverage the power of Referral Marketing; look for opportunities in your every day encounters and be diligent to keep developing a larger team that you can give and receive referrals.

Now we are ready to talk about Estimating and Selling your Projects.

Chapter 4

Selling Projects and Job Estimating

SELLING PROJECTS AND JOB ESTIMATING

No matter how amazing Artificial Grass is; no matter what consumers think of Artificial Grass; you must sell the project for your business to grow and thrive. Establishing a good reputation with the public in general through good customer service and the methods discussed in the Marketing Section earlier. What I want to cover in this section is all of the wisdom you will need once you are talking with an interested prospect.

Whether you are only on the phone or meeting with them in person; there are certain avenues you want to pursue and some good practices you will want to incorporate in your sales approaches that will help you have the best chance to gain that profitable installation project.

Qualifying a prospect: It is crucial to maximize your time. In order to allow for as many sales/estimating appointments as possible, do not be afraid to get an idea of whether the prospect is realistic about the cost of an Artificial Grass installation when you are first talking with them. Also, if they are only going to be quoting a small project area; then the whole sales transaction would best handled on the phone.

If the customer has a smaller job for you; you can explain that the smaller projects are more costly per square foot than larger projects because there are fixed costs involved in bringing your crew out to the site. The benefit of this strategy is that the prospect may decide to add more sections and areas to the project. There is no use in burning time and gas meeting with a prospect that will not have the budget to start a project with you. Ask your prospect, "Assuming you liked an estimate to install a new Artificial Grass lawn, when would you hope to start the project." After you find out how many square feet they are looking to get a quote on, and their timeframe for starting the project, you could have a conversation that might go something like this:

"Mr. Customer, many people I talk with about Artificial Grass are unfamiliar with the costs and benefits of this option. I wanted to make sure that you have an idea of the range of pricing you can expect, does that make sense?" "What have you heard about the costs involved in installing Artificial Grass?" This is a good time to introduce the comparison of square foot pricing on cement or paving stones. Artificial grass can be seen as a more affordable and better option over other "hardscape" options.

Preparing for the Appointment: Let me talk about being prepared for the sales appointment. Be sure you are presenting a professional image. This means good hygiene; arrive at the appointment well groomed and in quality business casual dress. This will help your prospect believe you are competent and add value to your product. This also applies to your truck and any equipment or supplies that you are using during the estimate and sales presentation. If you appear disheveled and messy than your prospect will quickly start loosing confidence and will stop being comfortable. It is easier to believe that you won't take good care of the details of the installation project.

You will need to bring a writing pad with some drawing paper (see exhibit xx) so you will be able to do a rough sketch of the Pattern (Installation area) you will be installing. Bring a calculator for doing your calculations. Bring a measuring tape and/or measuring wheel for measuring all the sides of the Pattern. Also, it will be good to have an organized set of samples for them to select an Artificial Grass choice from.

When you first start, you will want to have a list of questions that you will want to make sure and cover with each prospect.

SELLING PROJECTS AND JOB ESTIMATING

A good progression for every Estimate/Sales Presentation:

- Greeting and Warm-up: Make sure to take the time to give your prospect a warm greeting. It is always a good use of time to try to make a connection with your prospect. Some prospects may want take more time to get to know you. Definitely cooperate since they are the type of buyer that will not agree to an Installation project until they trust you and a long conversation is their process. Still, it is a good thing to sincerely compliment a prospect on some aspect of their home or neighborhood and get them in a brief and comfortable conversation.

- Introduce the process you want to complete. To help your prospect feel comfortable you can give them an idea of the steps you want to take to get them an estimate and answer their questions. Tell them that you will survey the area and get the information you need and then depending on the particulars you be able to prepare a quote for them before you leave.

- Ask for them to show you the areas where they want to install Artificial Grass. While you start measuring out and drawing the area; begin asking them questions about the project. Use the forms from the back of this book. This is an excellent time for testing to see if the customer has a timeframe and budget. You can be very assumptive about them wanting to proceed and "Trial" closing the sale.

- Based on their answers to the Estimating questions you will be able to show them various samples of Artificial Grass for them to select from. Also, you may want to discuss some of the options for other landscaping features like walking stones (capstones) or other special borders around trees or brush.

- Prepare the quote: Once you know the Square Footage and the Linear Feet around the pattern(s) you will then be able to use the Quoting Tool that will allow you to know the right type of Artificial Grass and prepare the supply costs involved. You will know what seaming or weed barrier, other supply costs you have based on how you are going to need seams. Follow the instructions for quoting.

- Sales Presentation: Before talking about specifics costs, you will want to build value with your prospect. A good place to start is by showing your prospect some "Before and After" pictures so that they can get a sense of how amazing their yard can look when you are done with the project you are proposing.

- You will want to discuss the process of installation. This will help your prospect understand about some of the difficulties that you are handling for them and add value to the cost of installation.

- You will want to build up their confidence in your company; talk about reference accounts you have. At the beginning that may be free accounts you help your friends install. Also, you will want to talk about how much of your business is based on referrals from satisfied customers. You will want to emphasize your commitment to satisfaction and your membership with the Better Business Bureau and other service, business groups.

- Now you are ready to present your pricing…

Presenting Pricing to the Prospect: My experience is that most people don't want to engage in negotiating. They just want you to be sincere and fair. If you are open about the efforts and costs necessary to do a great job for them and you maintain a comfortable selling atmosphere you will very likely win a new customer. Also, that new customer will be generous with referring their friends since they will be confident that you will not "hard sell" them.

A word about low prices: Most all the time, what I do in my presentation is start with the most affordable options for Artificial Grass. For example, a very affordable 50 ounce Artificial Grass selection will work well if they are not going to be very active in the yard and it will be mostly for show.

Remember to not be timid. You are comparing your Artificial Grass option with other paving or "hardscape" options; and those options are much higher per square foot.

I would advise you to not make it your goal to be the low price leader for your area. Do not lose sight of your major objective - to make a client while you make a profit. Anyone can produce a large sales volume selling dollar bills for ninety cents. But that will not last long. So keep control of your costs, and price your product carefully and keep your customers happy with quality service and Artificial Turf selections.

There is another school of thought when presenting pricing. Presentation techniques that were developed in the home improvement industry. The Salesman will use a series of questions to try to discover what the prospect is expecting to pay. You will then come in with a much higher figure so that the prospect then may be willing to raise their expected price that they were willing to pay. Then you will "close" the prospect by coming down close to their new expected price. If that is a style you would like to use, I would encourage you to seek out materials that teach those methods.

On occasion, I do find that I am presenting to someone that I suspect will need to negotiate my price down to be satisfied. So I will add some margin in my price for them to "win" from me. However, I typically use the other methods described above.

It is easy for me to discuss the advantages and performance of more expensive selections and then allow the customer to make a decision based on their budget. Many times I have found that prospects will want to entertain buying a job they can't afford; but I would rather they see me as a consultant that is showing them what I recommend and also other options and choices they can consider. I always make the choices clear and simple for them to understand. This will help prevent them from needing to think about the decision and postponing a start.

Something that is unique about the Artificial Grass industry is that your costs are not just dictated by the higher quality of your Artificial Grass and supplies. Your costs will be higher because you are choosing to use materials that are more environmentally responsible. There are ways to lower costs using materials that are more widely available because of this bad stigma. They do have lower costs; however, you will be sacrificing a commitment to being responsible to conserving the earth's resources. You can share these options with the customer and build value and higher integrity with them.

As you do more estimates you will become more comfortable watching for signals that the customer is interested and wanting to quickly move to authorizing an Agreement and giving you a deposit.

 **BIG TIP:** It is very important that you remember that showing your customer the <u>samples of the turf</u> will win many more projects for your company than giving them a very solid Return on Investment. In  my experience, after the customer has the desire to get Artificial Grass installed; a strong Return on Investment may help them justify the expense to an unenthusiastic spouse.

So here is a good Return on Investment Analysis you can develop.

8 Year Return on Investment Analysis

| Artificial Grass Lawn
Square Feet: 1000 | | Natural Sod Grass Lawn
Square Feet: 1000 | | |

Artificial Grass Lawn
   Square Feet: 1000

Natural Sod Grass Lawn
   Square Feet: 1000

| Initial Installation Cost | $9.00 | Initial Installation Cost | $2.00 |
| Initials Investment | $9000 | Initials Investment | $2000 |

Recommended maintenance on Artificial Grass is one annual Tune-up and disinfectant wash and spraying $400

Recommended maintenance on Natural Sod Grass:

	Month	Year
Water*	$100	$1200
Maintenance	$80	$960
Fertilizers		$100
Chemicals		$100
Irrigation Repairs*		$150
Total		$2510

Install Grass Yourself and save up to 40% off

| Total | $400 |

Initial Investment	$9000		Initial Investment	$2000
	Yearly	Total		Yearly	Total
Year 1	$400	$9,400	Year 1	$2,510	$4,510
Year 2	$400	$9,800	Year 2	$2,510	$7,020
Year 3	$400	$10,200	Year 3	$2,510	$9,530
Year 4	$400	$10,600	Year 4	$2,510	$12,040
Year 5	$400	$11,000	Year 5	$2,510	$14,550
Year 6	$400	$11,400	Year 6	$2,510	$17,060
Year 7	$400	$11,800	Year 7	$2,510	$19,570
Year 8	$400	$12,200	Year 8	$2,510	$22,080

Savings: $9,880 * Breakeven in the 4th Year!

*This analysis does not include a likely Re-investment in New SOD Lawn of $2000 after the 4th year. Also, the analysis understates typical water and repair costs. Finally, remember the Appreciation added to your property value!

SELLING PROJECTS AND JOB ESTIMATING

Return on Investment: If you are presenting to a prospect who will be replacing their natural lawn; this is an important part of presenting in the Artificial Grass Industry. You need to be able to become comfortable showing them the many costs that they will not have any longer after they have their new Artificial Grass lawn. The math is rather simple. You take their estimated costs for maintaining their current natural lawn. You will subtract all the costs they will no longer have to derive the monthly savings. This monthly savings is divided by the Installation Project costs to determine the Return of their investment.

If I have qualified them accurately and know that they want to start the project as soon as they have a good design and quote then I am very assumptive about how I describe the project and finish my presentation talking about the steps for starting a project with my company. Then I will do a "trial close" by asking a question that they would need to decide if they were planning to move forward.

Being presumptive in your sales approach will serve your prospect in two ways. First, if you are confident that you will be able to provide an excellent service and installation for your prospect; they need to read that in your manner. If you will not ask for the project; it can create unnecessary doubt in the prospects mind.

Secondly, your prospect will not become more interested and gain even more drive to move forward with a project after you leave the appointment. While you are there and they have all the details in front of them is the best time for them to decide. Many people talk about buyer's remorse; where a customer quickly regrets a decision. However, I want to talk about "buyer's relief." If your company can give them assurances that you are going to over-deliver and you are providing a quality proposal; that prospect needs your help to decide. Once they have decided they will be, and should be relieved.

Keep your Prospect Comfortable: If they are reluctant to answer the trial closing question then I will take the conversation back to some issues regarding their project and probe them for any more questions and be patient and calm.

If they start to run out of questions then I will ask them in a very unthreatening way. "Where would you like to take it from here?"

"I want to Think about it: This is the phrase that most sales people will seize up with. What your prospect is telling you is that you have not given them enough reasons and value to motivate them to move forward.   All you should do is to tell them that you understand and that it may be helpful for them to think about the project with you while you review some details. Then you should make a nice simple summary of all the highlights and benefits.   Ask the prospect about their concerns. If they are quiet, start to list possible objections.

If it is the price then I confirm that there are no other objections. I then attempt to find options. Maybe there are adjustments to the Artificial Grass selection. Maybe a larger project can be split in to smaller projects. If your prospect is a real handyman they may like to help with the preparation of the site in exchange for a lower price. Maybe there are some financing options that could be considered.   Be creative and remain in the role of the consultant.

Do be sure and tell your customer about rebates that may be available through their water board. You may want to have a list of the local agencies and contact information prepared for them so they can inquire and make the proper applications. It is important to not make promises about rebates since many prospects will make you responsible for the results and it will create customer service problems and

After you are contracting for your services you may want to delve into other home improvement projects that will result in co-marketing opportunities. I would recommend that unless the improvement is directly linked with your installation that you make a note of it and talk about it with them once your project is started.

A profitable and valuable objective is to be organized with all your contacts. Make sure you can easily find contact information for your customers, vendors, and co-marketing partners. Take good notes about each of these contacts so you can always be networking and more easily helping others get the help they need and return you the favor.

Intentionally Left Blank

Chapter 5

Operations and Customer Service

OPERATIONS AND CUSTOMER SERVICE

I have discovered in my years of installing that every installation is important. Because you focus on delivering a great service and product in each project you do, some of these customers will be setting up very profitable referral contacts for you. I have continually been surprised by which customers will provide the most profitable referrals and references.

Manage every installation like you are installing in your own home. Whether you doing every install yourself or you have work crews and managers you need to make sure to put your stamp of approval on the process and never allow substandard quality. Some important areas of an installation include:

1) Remember to have good compaction so there is no Grade Failure
2) Make sure the seams are done well.
Tip: Don't overstock your Glues and adhesives. Only keep enough for a few jobs on hand. So that you can be assured of good performance, make sure they are not over 90 days old.
3) Make sure grass has good grip and is tethered well to the ground

The key for high quality customer service is managing your new customer's expectations from the start and at every point of contact. Attempt to under promise and over deliver; or at least meeting the level of service that your client expects. At the point of starting a project, clearly review the steps and activities for installing their new Artificial Grass lawn.

If during the project you encounter any delays or details that have not been discussed; call in advance of delays and take the time to explain any issues. Solicit any feedback or comments from them; in case they feel shy to express concerns.

OPERATIONS AND CUSTOMER SERVICE

Make sure you and any of your work crew wear comfortable uniform shirts for the professional look. In order to make a good impression, make sure all tools and equipment, rented or otherwise, are kept nice and tidy as well.

After you have installed the project you can create a good impression by doing these two things. First, power wash the area so that your customer gets to see their new Artificial Grass lawn without any debris and installation related mess. Secondly, I would suggest you give your customer a checklist of Maintenance Instructions (with your business information all over it, of course). As you are reviewing these items, present your customer with some "complimentary" Artificial Grass from the Lot you installed for any possible repair needs they may have. Make sure the roll is marked clearly with your business information as well.

Some good income generating services to include in your Operations:

Artificial Grass Rejuvenation Team: Set up an efficient system to be able to service your customer's lawn. This could also be advertised to service existing Artificial Grass installations. Since you are their Rejuvenation service, you will be the business they think of when friends ask about their lawn and when they are ready to do other projects. You can distinguish your Installation by including the first service complimentary in your bids.

Become a Trainer: As other contractors you are networking with want to learn more; you can begin training them in a hands-on class format. You may want to offer to become a trainer who will come to the site and instruct their crews. This type of service could even be offered to a homeowner that wants to install the Artificial Grass but wants your services to oversee that work is done properly.

Intentionally Left Blank

Special Section

- Artificial Grass Vendors and Suppliers
- Installing Putting Greens
- Industry Information

MANUFACTURERS AND SUPPLIERS

Artificial Grass Manufacturer and Suppliers

NOTES:

EcoAlliance
www.ecosyntheticturf.com
www.ecoalliance.com
(866)326-2554
500 N. Sequoia Avenue
Ontario, CA 91761
USA

Greenfields: Sports Turf Systems
www.green-fields.nl
info@green-fields.nl
31(0)38 3372010
8260 Al Kampen
The Netherlands

CCG
www.ccgrass.com
info@ccgrass.com
86 25 86556235
Floor 5, Sports Center Business Bldg
No. 1-6 Wutaishan, Nanjing 210029
China

Limonta Sport
www.limontasport.com
area.com@limontasport.com
39 035 4812111
Via Crema, 60 24055 Cologno al Serio
Italy

MANUFACTURERS AND SUPPLIERS

Artificial Grass Manufacturer and Suppliers (Continued)

NOTES:

Act Global Sports
www.actglobalsports.com
Americas@actglobalsports.com
(512) 733-5300
4616 W Howard Lane, Suite 650
Austin, TX 78728 USA

Polytan
www.Polytan.de
info@polytan.com
49 0 8432 870
Gewerbering 3, D-86666 Burgheim
Germany

Italgreen
www.italgreen.it
info@italgreen.it
39 035 78 41 78
Via Crusnigo, 11-24030 Villa d'Adda
Italy

RadiGreen
www.radigreen.com
39 035 715911
24020 Gandino(BG)
Italy

MANUFACTURERS AND SUPPLIERS

Artificial Grass Manufacturer and Suppliers (Continued)

NOTES:

Playrite (Europe)
www.play-rite.co.uk
info@play-rite.co.uk
44 (0) 1924 412488
Wellington Mills, Liversedge
West Yorkshire WF 157FH
United Kingdom

Challenger Industries
www.challengerind.com
info@challengerind.com
(800)334-8873
205 Boring Drive
Dalton, GA 30721
USA

TenCate Grass (North America)
www.tencate.com
(423)847-8400
1131 Broadway Street
Dayton, TN 37321
USA

TigerTurf / Act Global Sports
www.tigerturfworld.com/na
(512)782-8175
4616 W. Howard Lane
Bldg 6, Suite 600
Austin, TX
USA

Artificial Grass Manufacturer and Suppliers (Continued)

NOTES:

Advanced Sports Installations
www.sportsinstallations.com
info@sportsinstallations.com
Formations House, 29 Harley Street
London W1G 9QR
Great Britain

Sportisca   (No-Infill Turf)
www.sportisca.com
41 71 365 62 62
Schwagalpstr 111, CH-9107 Urnasch
Switzerland

Trofil Sport bodensystem
www.trofil-sport.eu
49 2242 93388 0
Lohestrabe 40, D-53773 Hennef
Germany

Bonar Yarns
www.bonaryarns.com
44 (0) 1382 346 106
Caldrum Works, St Salvador Street
Dundee, DD3 7EU
United Kindom

Champion Grass (Distributor for TenCate and Bonar)
www.championgrass.com
719 Catalina Crescent
Burlington, Ontario L7L 5B9
Canada

MANUFACTURERS AND SUPPLIERS

Artificial Grass Manufacturer and Suppliers (Continued)

NOTES:

Rosehill Polymers
www.rosehill-polymers.ltd.uk
44 (0) 1422 829610
Villa Street, Off Beech Road
Sowerby Bridge, West Yorskshire HX6 2JT
United Kingdom

Saltex
www.saltex.fi
saltex@saltex.fi
385 6 557 0700
Sahatie 1
FI-62900 Alajarvi
Finland

Shaoxing Aladdin Enterprise
www.Aladdinturf.com
86 575 85146216
1505 Yanguang Bldg, Shengli Lu
Shaoxing 312000, Zhejiang
China

Playrite Sport Surfaces
www.play-ritesportsurfaces.com
(865)584-2818
7220 Coleridge Drive
Knoxville, TN 37919
USA

MANUFACTURERS AND SUPPLIERS

Artificial Grass Manufacturer and Suppliers (Continued)

NOTES:

Lano Sports
www.lanosports.com
32 (0) 56 65 42 90
Zuidstraat 44, 8530 Harelbeke
Belgium

Leling Taishan Artificial Grass
http://taishanturf.en.alibaba.com
0086-10-84985477
Room B307,B308 of Building 1, No 8
Beichendonglu, Chaoyang District Beijing
China

Guangzhou Sailling Sport Equipment
www.ecvv.com/company/sallingsport/
Rm1001, West Tower Yuan
Yang Ming Zhu Building, No. 21,
Hua Li Road, Cbd Zhu Jiang
New Town, Guangzh
China

Condor Grass
www.condorcompany.eu
31 38-4778911
Randweg14,8061 RW
P.O. Box 21, 8060AA, Hasselt
The Netherlands

MANUFACTURERS AND SUPPLIERS

Artificial Grass Manufacturer and Suppliers (Continued)

Desso Sports
www.dessosports.com/en/
0032 (0) 52 262 411
Robert Ramlotstraat 89, 9200 Dendermonde
Belgium

Artificial Grass Maintenance Products

Pioneer
www.pioneerathletics.com
(800)877-1500
5429 Industrial Parkway
Cleveland, OH 44135
USA

In-Fill Products

EcoAlliance
www.ecosyntheticturf.com
www.ecoalliance.com
(866)326-2554
500 N. Sequoia Avenue
Ontario, CA 91761
USA

NOTES:
_____
_____
_____
_____
_____
_____
_____
_____
_____
_____
_____
_____
_____
_____
_____
_____
_____
_____
_____
_____
_____
_____
_____
_____
_____
_____
_____
_____

MANUFACTURERS AND SUPPLIERS

In-Fill Products

NOTES:

EcoAlliance
www.ecosyntheticturf.com
www.ecowaterlessgrass.com
(866)326-2554
500 Sequoia Avenue
Ontario, CA 91761
USA

Eximlink
www.eximlink.com
info@eximlink.com
43 1 929 15020
Otto Bauer Gasse 24 3 26
1060 Wien
Austria

Limonta Sport
www.limontasport.com
area.com@limontasport.com
39 035 4812111
Via Crema, 60 24055 Cologno al Serio
Italy

Regalfill
www.regalfill.com
info@regalfill.com
86 519 85126201
#22 TianShan Road, Xinbel District
ChangZhou JiangSu
China

MANUFACTURERS AND SUPPLIERS

In-Fill Products continued

NOTES:

Unirubber
www.unirubber.com.pl
Unicom@unirubber.com.pl
48 75 772 10 00
Zielonka 17, 59-940 Wegliniec
Poland

Sibelco Sports & Leisure
www.Sibelcosportsandleisure.com
SCR-Sibelco NV - Quellinstraat 49, B-2018 Antwerpen
RPR Antwerpen BTW BE 0404.679.941 ING 320-0004270-72

Re-Tyre Lommel (Recyled In-Fill)
www.re-tyre.com
32 (0)11 552984
Industriezone Maatheide 66
3920 Lommel
Belgium

Gezolan AG
www.gezolan.ch/e/frame.htm
41 (0) 62 748 30 40
Werkstrasse 30, CH-6252 Dagmersellen
Switzerland

Granuflex
www.granuflex.com
31 (0) 20 4978201
Sicilieweg 20, 1045 AS Amsterdam
The Netherlands

In-Fill Products continued

Mineral Visions Inc. (Flex Sand)
www.flexsand.com
(800) 255-7263
11830 Ravenna Road
Chardon, OH 44024
USA

Specialty Products

Terraplas (AG Coatings – Anti-Icing)
www.terraplas.com
44 (0) 1332 812813
Hall Farm House, High Street
Castle Donington, Derby DE742PP
United Kingdom

Mondo Grass (Artificial Plants for Landscape)
www.mondograss.com
491 Masters Way
Athens, GA 30607
USA

Intentionally Left Blank

Installing a Putting Green

One of the more popular uses of Artificial Grass will be your Putting Green installations. Many clients will be looking for a chance to go to their back yard and relax while working on their putting skills.

Some will even want to create a surface to Pitch a ball onto their Putting Green. You will want to advise your client to keep the Pitching area within 15 yards of their Putting Green since the ball will always bounce off. Also, it will be noticeable to many golfers that the Artificial Putting surface will not roll as fast as the Natural grass at their favorite golf course. So let us design and install the Putting Green!

Purchasing Supplies

<u>Base</u>: Putting Greens require that you use Decomposed Granite (Ask for "Fines"). You need to be very careful to not create imperfections in the base and DG will help assure you have a smooth result.

<u>Turf</u>: 3/4 inch or 1/2 inch Nylon will be your best choices.

<u>InFill</u>: Very fine "Clean Sand" (90 Grit) Make sure it is not Sub-Angular sand which will create a very hard bounce for customers that want to pitch onto the Putting green. You will only need about 1/2 pound per square foot. If you are going to be chipping onto the Putting Green use more In-fill to create a softer bounce.

<u>Practice Green Cup</u>: Depending on the size of the Putting Green the client may want to purchase several sets of Cups and Flag Poles.

<u>Supplies</u>: Nails and Adhesive will be necessary.

<u>Prepare and excavating the area</u> will be similar to a regular Artificial Grass install. One difference will be that you will be cementing in your Putting Green Cups. You will want to locate any Cups 30" from any of the edges.

Another difference is that you will need the necessary time to make sure that your final compacted area is very smooth and free of any rough areas where the grade changes.

A final difference is that you will be sizing your Bend-a-Board to frame in the Putting Green Pattern after you have completed the measuring and laying of your Putting Green.

Preparing your Pattern and Cutting the Artificial Turf: Now you are ready to Cut your Artificial turf:

1. Cover your Putting Green area with a Weed Barrier. Partially Nail down the Weed Barrier with Nails about every 6 inches. After you draw your Pattern you will be removing the nails.

2. Draw your Putting Green Pattern on the Weed Barrier surface.

3. Cut out the Pattern you marked off with about 1 inch of extra barrier on the edges. Mark this piece of Weed Barrier "Top."

4. Now Roll out your Artificial Grass on a flat smooth surface with the Green Turf facing down.

5. Flip over your Weed Barrier Pattern and place on "Top" so it is facing the Black Backing of your Artificial Turf. This is done so that your Artificial Turf will be the pattern you designed when you flip it over to install.

6. Using Duct Tape you will tape the Weed Barrier Pattern at the edges of the Artificial Grass roll and now be able to use the Pattern to cut the Artificial Turf to its approximate shape and dimension.

First you can lay down the Weed Barrier into the Pattern. Only use nails on the edges. Now you can take your Artificial Turf and place it down in the Pattern. With Putting Greens you will only be using nails on the edges. You will use some nails on the edges to temporarily hold the Artificial Turf while you start to anchor it to the Pattern.

The next step is to take your Clean Sand Infill and start to lay it into the middle of the Putting Green area. You will want to be very careful to lay a small portion of Infill and then brush it in well.

The reason you are going to start in the middle area is so that the weight of the Infill will cause the Artificial Turf to start to lay snug against the base of the Pattern.

Keep applying and brushing in your Clean Sand into the middle areas. Now you are ready to go around the edges of your Pattern and trim away the extra Artificial Turf to create a very straight and clean cut. As always, you will fold back the turf and cut and trim from the back side.

Before you start to do your final anchoring down of the turf you will want to locate the Putting Green Cups. Start by cutting an "X" shape in the middle of the Cup. Then trim in a circle just 1/8 of an inch inside the cup. Then you will stretch the turf open and pull behind the lip of the cup.

With your Artificial turf weighted down; now you can trim the edges to the proper length; apply your adhesive and lay your edges down. At the edges you will be able to nail down those edges or tuck them into Benderboard as designed.

Your now ready to complete the laying of Infill on the outer edges by applying the Infill evenly and brushing as before. You will want to apply water to help any residual Infill filter deep into the turf.

Now you are ready to enjoy your new Putting Green!

Intentionally Left Blank

INDUSTRY INFORMATION

Training and Continuing Education

Besides the training you are getting in this book you will want to continue to learn and improve your skills and understanding of the Artificial Grass industry. Below are two possible training options to consider:
http://www.ecoalliance.com/become-an-installer.php
Southern California
http://www.asgi.us/asgicertified/
Sacramento, CA (web based)

A third option would be to do an internet search in your region and look at both Artificial Turf suppliers or distributors that would want you to buy their turf and would be glad to train you in installation. Below are examples in my area out here in California.
http://www.prolawnturf.com/content/training_program.html
Supplier inTemecula, CA
http://www.playfieldusa.com/
Arizona Distributor

A fourth option is to network with other Artificial Turf Installers that are just out of your region and could easily become an installer that you would exchange referrals with. You could take the opportunity to spend time working and learning on their installation projects.

You can stay current on the industry directions by subscribing to newsletters or bulletins offered by the Manufacturers listed on Page XX I highly recommend these four websites:

Landscape Contractor
www.**landscape**online.com

Landscape Architech
www.asla.org

Sythetic Turf Council newsletter
www.**syntheticturfcouncil**.org

Turf Field
www.turfmagazine.com

Industry Terms and Important Concepts

Similar to carpeting, Artificial Grass is made up of Blades that are created by the stitching of various yarns to a backing. The Yarns are made from a substance known as Olefin. These yarns are used to create the various turfs by stitching them to various types of backings. You will see turfs that are stitched from three

Nylon	PolyPropolene PP	PolyEtholyne (PE)
UV Protection Sprayed On	UV Protection Mixed Into Production of Yarn	Same as (PP)
Absorbs Water Or Urine (Poor for Kennels) (Poor for Kennels)	Doesn't Absorb Water Doesn't Absorb Chemicals Dries quickly Stain Resistant Fade Resistant	Same as (PP) Same as (PP) Same as (PP) Same as (PP) Same as (PP)
	More Ridged Freezes Under 50 degrees	Softer Good for cold conditions

These three types of yarns are manufactured: Split Film, Mono Filament, or Mono Tape. By forming them in different shapes they can be cut or "texturized" to add a variety of Turf designs. In the end, the cost of your turf is a function of how much of the yarn and backing materials are used and how much processing time the manufacturer uses. So you will see variations on these specifications

Stitch count	Stitch gauge	Row gauge
Face Weight	Primary backing	Secondary Backing

Also, the Strength of a turf can be described in different ways:
- Tensile Strength: try to pull it
- Compression strength: try to compress it
- Flexural Strength: try to bend or flex it
- Torsional Strength: try to twist it
- Impact Strength: strike it sharply and suddenly

INDUSTRY INFORMATION

Take full advantage of the many training and educational resources and keep learning all the time. Here are some industry vocabulary and areas to get further training and learn about as you are gaining more experience.

- Type of Yarn - classic slit film, tape, monofilament using three types of materials: Poly Ethylene, Poly Propylene, and Nylon

- How yarns are made — Texturizing yarns

- Stitch count and Stitch guage

- Row gauge

- Tufting and Tufted points

- Face Weight

- Tuft bind

- Primary and Secondary backing

- Salvage and Denier

- Grain or nap of surface (face)

- Inline seams ; Tail - butt or cross seams

- UV Protection

- Blade Height

- Infills and Rubber Crumb issues (Lead-Free Certificates)

This is a useful form that will help you draw the Pattern and keep a record of items and supplies to cost out for your Estimate:

Put Your LOGO and Address/Telephone Here

Name: _____
Address: _____
_____
Phone: _____

S/F: _____
Demo _____
Difficult Access: _____
Sawcuts: _____
Base Prep: 2" 4" 6" 8" _____
Evacuation & Grading: _____
Drains: _____
Extras: _____
Cups: _____
Putting Green: _____
Stakes: _____
Brock Or AGS of So CA BASE: _____
Linear Ft of Framing: _____
Infill Type: _____
Source: _____
Manufaturer: _____
Paver/Sod Name: _____
Color: _____
Price Per Sq. Ft. _____
Standard: Custom
Pattern: _____
Border: _____
Color: _____
Perimeter L/F: _____
Homeowner Approval: _____
Date: _____

This is a useful form that will help you create a Project Budget and Cost

ARTIFICIAL GRASS SOLUTIONS OF SOUTHERN CALIFORNIA

Job Name: _____   Bid Date: _____

	Square Foot	Unit Cost		Price
Demolition:				
☐ Grass Tractor (for 3" Base)		x $1.85	=	
☐ Grass Hand Removal (3" Base)		x $2.25	=	
☐ Clean Dirt Removal (3" Base)		x $1.66	=	
☐ Grass Hand Removal (Eco)		x $1.00	=	
☐ Clean Dirt Removal (Eco)		x $0.85	=	
Backyard Access:				
☐ Upcharge		x $1.10	=	
☐ Hand Carry Access Only		Bid Only		Must be able to use wheelbarrow. (slopes, stairs, excessive distance?)
Base:				
☐ 3"		x $0.80	=	
☐ Eco Base		x $1.65	=	
Synthetic Sod:				
☐ Eco Delux		x $2.50	=	
☐ Eco Elite		x $3.20	=	
☐ Eco Perennial Rye		x $2.64	=	
☐ Eco California Plush		x $2.65	=	
☐ Eco Next Generation		x $3.03	=	
☐ Eco Next GenerationShort		x $2.40	=	
☐ Eco Rugby		x $3.48	=	
☐ Eco Rugby w/ Tan Thatch		x $3.53	=	
☐ Eco Putting Green 3/4		x $2.66	=	
Infill:				
☐ Play Sand		x $0.29	=	
☐ Coated Sand		x $0.75	=	
Supplies:				
☐ Stakes (plastic)		x $0.75	=	
☐ Benderboard		x $1.80	=	
☐ Staples		x $0.03	=	
☐ SeamTape				
☐ Seam Glue (5 gallon)		x $309.00	=	
☐ Weed Barrier				
☐ Nails - 5" (box)		x $70.47	=	
Drainage:				
☐ 4"		x $11.00	=	Under 100 l/F
☐ 4"		x $9.00	=	Min 100 l/F
Drain Covers:				
☐ Square Plastic		x $7.00	=	
☐ Round Plastic		x $5.00	=	
☐ Curb Core Under City Walk 3"		x $508.25	=	
☐ Curb Only		x $321.00	=	Permits by other - min $250
Paver Mow Strip:				
☐ Straight Running		x $12.84	=	
☐ Radius		x $14.98	=	
PVC Sleeves:				
☐ 2"		x $8.00	=	Lay in only, no tie-ins
Accessories:				
☐ Practice Green Cup (aluminum)		x $20.25	=	
☐ 24" Flag Pole		x $23.55	=	
☐ Red Flag		x $8.70	=	
☐ **MISC/ Extra**				
				TOTAL PRICE

5405 Alton Parkway, #A425, Irvine, CA 92604 • www.AGSartificialgrass.com • 877.886.8873

Made in the USA
San Bernardino, CA
05 March 2013